Can you hear the people sing?
Global responses to the Pandemic

Palewell Press

Can you hear the people sing?
Global responses to the Pandemic

Editor – Camilla Reeve

Can you hear the people sing? Global responses to the Pandemic

First edition 2020 from Palewell Press,
www.palewellpress.co.uk

Printed and bound in the UK

ISBN 978-1-911587-45-3

The cover photo of a woman clapping the NHS during the pandemic was taken by Guillus and downloaded from our image- suppliers at www.shutterstock.com

A CIP catalogue record for this title is available from the British Library

Acknowledgements

The Editor would like to thank everyone who helped in the production of this anthology including Kirstin Gentleman, who was our volunteer publishing assistant when we started compiling the anthology; and all the contributors for their inspiring words and for their enthusiasm and support throughout.

Dedication

This anthology is dedicated to everyone who died during the Covid-19 year, and to those who mourn them.

Contents

Foreword 1
ELSEWHERE ELSEWHEN 3
Lantern's Day 4
I'll Stay Home Now 6
In Lockdown 7
Lockdown III 8
Fire 10
Time of Corona 11
Stuck in a cycle 14
My San Quentin Death Row Coronavirus Experience 16
A strange sun 22
Corona Poem 25
Quarantine Diary: Day 64 26
Boukra 28
Can you hear the people sing? 35
UK LOCKDOWN BEGINS 37
Stay Lucky 38
Hopeful 40
The Fantastic Mr. Maj 41
The Postman 51
Front Doors 52
Hiding Myself 54
Day 83 58
Insomnia 59
Coronavirus 60

Something Wanting 61
The Flimsy 65
Sleeping with C19 66
708 today 67
It is the breath 68
NATURE REPRIEVED 71
It was as if 72
Wild flowers on May Day 74
Going Wild 75
The Return 76
At Ashton Court, Clifton 77
Thinking with the Hand 78
A Journey Around My Flat 79
Socrates awaiting 80
To the Quarantine 81
Walking Our Allotted Span – Colehill, Dorset 82
Gardening in lockdown 84
Coming Down 86
Social Distancing of Sparrows 87
LOSING TRACK OF TIME 89
Half-living through Lockdown 90
Arsenic and Pearls 91
All these weeks 92
A New Way of Living 93
Lockdown: Easter Sunday 94
The Ghost Inside 96

During the time of Corona 97
Making Marmalade in 2020 105
Blue 106
Night's Midpoint 107
Last Days 108
UK LOCKDOWN ENDS 109
Lockdown VI 110
I said No 111
Emerging: 2020 112
The Best Things In Life Are Free 113
The Bicycle Shed 114
My May 2020 Diary Excerpts and Ruminations 115
Summer Solstice 118
Dream 120
From March to Now 121
The Ghosts of Lockdown 122
FURTHER AHEAD 125
Something new 126
The Cave on the Moon 127
Lockdown or LOCKED IN? 129
Laughing behind a Mask 130
Sometimes I can't hold up the wreckage 132
Lockdown was easy – but what next? 133
Making a World One's Home 135
Prayer 136

REFERENCE 137

Pages where Authors' work appears 138

Author Biographies 140

Palewell Press 151

Foreword

When coronavirus reached the UK, I didn't realise how much it would affect my life, the economy and the whole of society. But I was determined, as far as I could, to deliver the book publication projects Palewell Press had promised while exploring new ways of doing so. That choice helped me personally, providing contact with many of our wonderful writers as well as the artists who were generously collaborating with us.

As the NHS and other public service heroes risked their lives to protect all of us, I wondered what world would rise from the ashes of the pandemic. Lockdown offered a breathing space to think about the world we need, how to make it more fair and more sustainable. So I invited people to share their poems and prose about this challenging time and their ideas for the future. Receiving submissions to the anthology certainly brightened my spring and summer.

There were so many wonderful submissions from writers around the world, as well as from those living in the UK, that I make no apology for the size of this anthology. If you read carefully you may see contributors being inspired to write about the same subject, The pandemic has provided common experiences in communities throughout the world and led to a global meeting of minds.

Going through Lockdown felt endless – like a train journey through a strange country without mountains or other landmarks, and whose station names were in an alien script. But suddenly Lockdown was coming to an end. I can't have been alone in feeling nervous at moving out of quarantine.

Two comments from Palewell authors helped me. Frank McMahon wrote "It is very difficult to know how best to influence the new normal. Perhaps easiest is to start at a personal level by renewing actual contact with family and friends and talking about they and you have coped, survived, perhaps prospered (not necessarily in a financial way)." And Helen Boyles shared her feeling of awe at "the solidarity that people have maintained as well as of the self-sacrificing generosity and hard work of so many besides key workers."

Covid-19 issued a clarion call for us to help the vulnerable and be more aware of the needs of those around us. And as we look ahead, we can't ignore the increasingly urgent and interlinked challenges of climate change and the refugee crisis. I'm proud of the international scope of the anthology and hope its wonderfully wide range of insights will contribute to a creative debate about our future.

Camilla Reeve

ELSEWHERE ELSEWHEN

Lantern's Day

Balcony. Tall building.
A basin bangs in cold air.
A woman cries out.
For her infected mother.
For a hospital bed.

Save life! Save life!
I can't do it.
Anyone's coming?
I don't know what I can do.
Who can help? Help me.

Catch wall-climbers.
Block VPNs.
Cancel their WeChat accounts. For life.
A ban freezes River Han.

Lanterns are muzzled.
Ghosts wander.
Lovers make reunion rice-balls.
In separate rooms.
And dine on screen.

A mobile stays on mute.
Owner unknown.
What is touched inside?

I continue to write.
With my firestick.
In stove.
My red dress swirls around.

Sulfur dioxide level reaches 1700mg.
Body bags rush out of textile factories.
Cremators are hurried.
From neighbouring provinces.
Three dead children zip in one bag.

She dares not go home.
Like fellow nurses. Or doctors.
Nor dares she let husband give her a ride.
From hostel to hospital, she walks.
In the dark.

He follows.
In his car.
Head-lights
Light up her road ahead.

Yan Li

I'll Stay Home Now

I know what I'm doing.
I'll look after myself.
We just don't' have enough hands.
Nor enough gloves.

Make me another mask.
If you have to.
And a few gowns.
I'll share them.

Sure, I'm scared.
I could bring it home.
I know you're worried for me.
I'm also worried for you.

Patients are dying. Alone.
Some of us, too.
Loved ones aren't allowed to come.
They say I love you on the phone.

Don't cry.
This is what I do.
If it gets me,
Do not enter my room.

I'll stay home now.
I'll listen to you instead.
Don't take me to the hospital.
Don't want to take up a bed.

Yan Li

In Lockdown

We pray for the tide to turn, our grief and joy postpone.
Every day the news gets worse, we double our trust –
even this will pass, we cry, hanging on to our faith.

The natural order of life is change, we reckon.
Let's not forget it is darkest before dawn –
we sing in an uncertain world as we soldier on.

There is talk of shortages, of lives not worth saving –
the veneer of civilisation stripped in a heartbeat.
By now we know all the synonyms of despair.

Families bury their dead without ceremony.
For the frail and old abandoned in care homes
death arrives masked as a saviour.

Not knowing when the pandemic will be done,
what it will take for the virus to leave us alone –
we accept loneliness as a path to being human.

In lockdown nature recovers, humans struggle;
our lives, in their reincarnations, unrecognisable.
Some of us continue to dream of the impossible –

dream of transforming our one and only home,
this beautiful earth, where we may live and grow
together, learn to be part of a wonderful world.

Shanta Acharya

Lockdown III

It is not
that a three-day lockdown
is unbearable
beyond acceptable.
There are ordinary days
when I prefer
to leave my library
only when I desire
a beer on Aberdeen shore.
But by this third day of lockdown,
I find myself
feeling restless,
pulling my hair
and dripping with sweat
in front of a fan.
I realised
I should be outside
on my evening walk
along Aberdeen beach,
saying hello
to friends driving by,
children with trays of goods
who call me uncle,
and sensual sex workers
calling me darling
to loud tunes of afrobeat.

What makes this lockdown
difficult to bear
is knowing I am confined
in fear of a lethal virus.
Though I am not a prisoner,
I am not free,
because freedom is choice;
the option to stay in
or go out
as desired.

Joseph Kaifala

Fire

Lungs drowned by fire, too many, even one
too many. A ring of flame drives those closest
back, enfolds strangers drawn there by vocation.
Some have died and all are scarred, while we

offer rainbows and doorstep applause, cut
firebreaks between family and friends,
swerve round others in the shuttered streets
and close the distance with a nervous smile.

Figures are announced as if from a distant
war; graphs, projections, timelines. This war could
break upon our home at any time.
Its fire prowls. We are oxygen

and brushwood in this long, arid season.
Voices sound across the smoke. Where was
the water to dowse those early sparks? Who stood
down the firewatch? Who neglected history?

How many fewer? How many more?

Frank McMahon

Time of Corona

"How do you destroy a monster without becoming one?"

-1-

Rejection…
Out breaks the deadly Virus
With no address,
Speaks only the language of death
Knocks at the door
To invite me
Tangoing with it
Till the end

-2-

Coronation of loneliness...
Rain
Cloud and dew too
Plus this invisible, silent brute force
That takes away
The joy from me
And from my face

-3-

Unrestrained...
After all are gone
I start to chase
A naughty fly that carries a Virus
In the house
And I tiptoe back
Wrapped by an old blanket
To check my epidemic dreams
Of last night

/continued

-4-

Self-imposed isolation...
Too tired to work and think
I open the window
And wish to die
With the rose
Instead of by this unseen disease

-5-

Splendid culinary rave ...
With Almighty danger
My lips are absent
My mind is so busy
I asked: Are you there?
"Yes I will always be there"
Said my empty stomach

-6-

Thunderous silence...
Time spent
In a Ghost town
Sewing a net full of tears
And broken thoughts
Interrogating intensely
A bubble that I have seen
Gently rising to the surface
Of my cup of tea
In a deserted canteen

-7-

Vast vacuum...
In our new office
I sit with my boss
Together we do nothing
While the empty drawers
And the dark monitors
Say suitable prayers
In silent meditation

-8-

Rosy time...
From my little vase
On my desk
A flower says:
`I will permit my fragrance
To be the patron of the air
And an affective love virus
To defeat that cursed eclipse`
I will give it also
A sweet voice to sing
Happy tunes to brighten
The day

Ata Alsady

Stuck in a cycle

As it was told to me;
In a place filled with giants and ogres,
Where the ground cracked beneath every boot,
And the air smelled of decay.
Where LIFE itself did not enter.

In this place, the many were born one in division.

Their energy extracted to build.
They laboured and laboured,
Exhausted - they no longer resisted,
But began giving themselves away.

Further and further apart they grew.

Losing sight of each other,
As they could no longer see themselves.
LIFE decided to hover
And waited with bated breath.

Wanting to step in, but knowing,
life as they know it – would be no more.
She patiently waited, hoping they remembered,
But they grew further apart.

Sucked dry. Building. Burning.
The giants and ogres grew fatter and fatter.
And life in division grew into a web –
Turning cells into cells.

It flowed in and out of itself.

The old became new
And the new got old.
In and out of itself,
Stuck in a cycle.

Sucked dry. Building. Burning.
LIFE decided to hover
And waited with bated breath.
As the body kept falling apart.

Michelle Fuller

Footnote from author: *This poem was written in November 2019. Reading it now, it seems to speak directly to the current state of the world and where we are as a collective consciousness.*

My San Quentin Death Row Coronavirus Experience

In late January 2020, President Donald Trump was fully aware of the potential danger and present threat of Coronavirus, even as it would take the WHO until March 11 to declare a pandemic. In that same month, San Quentin prisoners received an administrative notification that one of the guards tested positive. At the time, I was not overly concerned because I was healthy and in good shape, but of course viruses, pathogens with the sole aim of wreaking havoc on healthy cells, don't care about that.

San Quentin's initial flimsy attempt to thwart the virus was to issue face masks, pass out hand sanitizer, cancel all visiting, halt movement except for emergencies, and split the recreational yard in half in an effort to limit the number of prisoners in close contact. These measures would fail completely.

In these early stages, rumors began circulating about outbreaks in other prisons, including The California Institute for Men (CIT), which turned out to be the epicenter of the California prison spread. But in early days, San Quentin was still relatively free of any Covid-19 cases. Unfortunately, under a court order, the California Department of Corrections and Rehabilitation on May 31 transferred 121 prisoners from CIT to *an already overcapacity and overcrowded* San Quentin.

Several of these transferred prisoners were put in quarantine the moment they stepped off the bus because they exhibited signs of Covid-19! Unsurprisingly, within a matter of days the virus spread wildly, infecting both inmates and guards in high numbers, leading to a lockdown of the prison.

In the second week of June I was transferred to East Block—a unit that houses most Death Row prisoners—and prisoners there were experiencing symptoms when I arrived. However, because the prison was not testing people in East Block at the point no one knew who was positive or negative. It was not until June 18 when staff announced over the intercom that testing for Covid-19 would be offered to all prisoners who wanted it, but testing was not mandatory. Most things in prison are, of course mandatory, so why not Covid-19 testing in the midst of an outbreak?

For me, getting a test was a no-brainer. I always want to know what's happening to my body, good or bad. On June 18 I was escorted into a long line of other death Row prisoners waiting in a small recreation yard to be tested. When my turn came up, I was directed to sit in a chair, with a guard posted behind me. To my left on two tables draped with a white cloth were spread medical paraphernalia. The two nurses present were outfitted in biohazard suits, looking like they were ready to inspect a contaminated lab.

"It's gonna be simple," one told me, as she asked my name and CDC number. "I will swab your throat first for five or six seconds and then your nostrils." She leaned over me, gently lifted up my mask, and inserted the Q-Tip in my throat, then my nostrils.

She was right; it was simple, and not painful. In fact, it sort of tickled and nearly made me laugh.

Later that evening, I felt a mild but irritating headache coming on. I wasn't alarmed but couldn't understand what brought it on. By the next morning, however, this mild headache became a major throbbing pain, which felt as if someone were bouncing basketballs inside my head, and I felt weak, like I was coming down with a bug, possibly the flu. I told myself I'd soldier through it, as I had done many times before. I figured once I did my daily exercises, I'd feel better. But I labored through my routine, uncharacteristically having to sit down and rest between sets, bending over with my hands on my knees, breathing hard through my mouth.

Over the next few days in incremental stages, I experienced a series of symptoms which, before my tests results came back, convinced me I was stricken with Covid-19. My headed pounded without respite for three days, the excruciating pain traveling back and forth between the crown of my head and forehead. When I placed my fingers on either spot it felt soft and tender, and I felt if I pressed down harder my fingers might sink into my skull. I developed a dry cough that got worse when I laid down, and experienced dramatic chills, shaking, and body aches.

My hands trembled like I was a junkie in need of a fix, and when I tried to hold a tumbler filled with water and raise it to my mouth my hand shook so much I had either to hold it with both hands or use a straw. I lost my appetite and my sense of taste, and my stomach felt bloated. I thought making one of my favorite breakfasts, oatmeal, might help, so I chopped up a banana and mixed it in with some peaches, trail mix, and a spoonful of peanut butter. But it tasted horrible, and I flushed it down the toilet. I wanted nothing more to do with food.

The extreme fatigue I felt was the worst, as if oxygen was constantly being sucked from my lungs. I would fall asleep around 7:00 pm and sleep for twelve hours, forcing myself out of bed each morning to walk a few steps back and forth in my narrow cell, and that was a challenge. I did not have the energy to read. Ultimately, and this went on for five or six days, I would stretch out on a wool blanket on the floor, cover myself with another blanket, and sleep off and on much of the day, which is uncommon for me.

While I was sick, I regularly heard the loud buzzard-like sound of the cellblock alarm go off, which is most often precipitated by a cadre of prisoners shouting in unison, "Man down, man down, man down!" along with the cell number of the person in distress. On a daily basis, people on the block were passing out and experiencing respiratory problems due to Covid-19. The worst cases were transferred to an outside hospital and placed on ventilators. Some never returned.

As of early September 2020, twenty-seven San Quentin prisoners have died from Covid-19 and over twenty-two hundred have tested positive. Nearly everyone who lived on my tier tested positive. A red sticker, the Covid-19 Scarlett Letter, was taped on the front of each of our cells.

Twice a day nurses stopped by my cell to ask if I wanted my temperature and oxygen checked. They also asked a series of other questions: Are you experiencing shortness of breath? Do you have a fever? Have you lost your taste and sense of smell? Do you have a cough or headache? Since I never reported a fever or shortness of breath, I was not considered to be in the danger zone.

The only advice I got from nurses was to drink plenty of water and to let the staff know of any changes in my symptoms. That's all they had for me. The medical staff had already bungled their job when they allowed prisoners in East Block who tested positive to stay in their cells instead of removing them immediately from the building or prison, if necessary, so my expectations were low. They tested us, but they didn't act accordingly. I understood that this was uncharted territory for the prison staff and medical personnel at San Quentin, but it was hard to understand the failure for the prison to follow basic protocol for slowing or stopping the spread of the virus.

My next-door neighbor and friend tested positive on the same day I did. He experienced several of the same symptoms, but his headache, chills, and body aches and coughing lasted only 24 hours, while it took two weeks for him to regain his lost sense of taste and smell. When I confided in him that I had avoided food for four days, he told me I should try eating some soup, and gave me two packets of Top Ramen. While even the idea of eating other food in my locker filled me with disgust, the prospect of soup appealed to me, taking me back to the days my mother served chicken or tomato soup to soothe me when I caught a cold, had a sore throat, or came down with a fever. The first spoonful went down with ease, and the second, third and fourth tasted even better. I saved the second packet; if I was on the mend, I didn't want to press my luck.

That night around 2:00 am I woke up drenched in sweat. My sheets and pillowcase were so wet I had to replace them with another set. I washed up, went back to sleep, and woke up a few hours later feeling rejuvenated. Within a couple of days, I was able to get back into my regular routine: the headaches, chills, body aches and coughing that had wracked my body were gone. Food was good again, and I felt as strong as ever. The latest reports suggest that symptoms can linger or reappear in different forms and that you can be reinfected, so I don't know if I'm completely out of the woods, and I don't expect San Quentin to vanquish the virus anytime soon. But I'm glad to be alive and well, along with everyone else in the world who has survived their encounter with this monstrosity.

The Coronavirus and Covid-19 remind me exactly how vulnerable I am, along with all the people on earth who live in poor communities without political influence or access to proper medical care. They also remind me, and should remind everyone, that we are all connected, no matter where we are; we share the same earth and our common humanity should inspire us to preserve it by taking good care of it, and of each other.

Steve Champion

A strange sun

Something new is amongst us, rising out of the viral ocean.
Shaking itself free, it floats into the air,
its reddish glow a strange sun,

a spoked wheel, its halo shining under a microscope: its crown.
We're in a blizzard of red dust blowing
every which way, a desert storm –

no point trying to drive on – stop the car. Sit in silence.
Sit in the heat. Keep the windows closed.
Don't scratch your eyes. Don't blow your nose.

This is the time to turn statue. The angel of death is passing over our doors
but now there's nothing to paint on them.
In their locked boxes the frail chatter quietly

to their tea-trays, to the pale shadows in corners that have always
been willing to listen. They know the air
is slowly leaving their rooms,

their once-buoyant balloons slowly shrinking. An old man stands,
totters to the window, presses his fingers
on the glass. Outside the car park is empty.

So many fingers star-fished on windows, faces half-seen, half-smiling:
mother to child, child to mother.
Voices clatter through letterboxes.

We are tied to ourselves now, adrift in a red sea, do not know
who we are inside masks and gowns,
only our eyes glow.

/continued

Screens conjure graphs, percentages, pictures of empty streets –
a razzle-dazzle ruckus –
anything to stave off our silence.

Meanwhile flowers stretch to the sky uninterrupted. I wake at dawn
to the blackbird calling to its many selves,
printing its song on the still-wet, newborn morning.

I listen to myself breathe. I put my hands over my heart, hold my breath,
hear someone drumming in the red tent –
a-live   *a-live*   *a-live.*

Sue Proffitt

Corona Poem

There's a wild virus on the loose,
Making people lose some screws,
Diving deep into oblivion and isolation,
Segregated existences, mutually confined,
Breathing carcinogens without knowing,
Passing diseases on like confetti,
Sprinkling germs into our nostrils,
Wishing fear away of infection,
Setting mutual aid communities up
In response to inadequate measures from the top,
We seek solace in our interactions
Whilst keeping up social distance,
A new contagious world lives on,
Breaking the system, blaming the sun.

Libaharan Ravindran

Quarantine Diary: Day 64

He says strawberries; I say seeds.
He says iris; I say sex.
He says faith; I cross myself with alcohol.

Two months of this Covid isolation and I'm plunged
into this greenscreen Zoom and WhatsApp existence—
the only witnesses to my lung–swelling
grunts, the circle of nervous black flies
I hunt with my yellow electric racket.

It takes only two AAs to fry the buzzing pests!
Who gave them permission to collect
under my ash tree in this city backyard?
Haven't they heard?
Gatherings are strictly forbidden.

He says have you no mercy? I say, let's party.

If I don't send them to their maker,
something else would. It's all pointless, anyway –
Isn't it?

That fly over there, the one I'm about to smack
has wandered into this flawless stream of light.
Perfect target.
Like us. Now. For God's golden racquet.

Smack!

He says madness, I say of course
it always starts with something slight,
like maple syrup dribbled on the blue
railing that separates our fruit bed
from the neighbor's; splattering the line
of clueless ants with the sharp
jet of water from the hose—
                    pointed, endless, without reason.

Sholeh Wolpé

Boukra

Five-months-and-thirteen-days since submission date

"Boukra! Tomorrow! When you're back we can select new paint colours together."

"I'm counting the hours *habibi*, my beloved. I was thinking one teal wall in... hello, hellooooo, Adel! Can you hear me?"

Yara shakes her phone, switches off her video. Tries to redial again. Until she admits defeat.

"Mummyy! I'm back! Is daddy online?" Layla, her sweet-soon-to-be-a-teenager-daughter has arrived. Yara takes a deep breath. She looks in the mirror, sees her own disappointed face. She forces a smile. Once more this week, she needs to explain.

"*Habibti*, my sweetheart! He was so excited to be seeing you, but the electricity cut just minutes before you arrived."

"But I ran fast. I thought there was still an hour! I really ran!" Layla's eyes welling in disappointment.

Layla hasn't seen her virtual father on the screen in over a week. Yara knows Layla has made a list of stories that she wants to tell her father. She smiles, puts her hand on Layla's cheek and says: "Remember, boukra-tomorrow, we're going home. The electricity won't matter. We'll be with him in the flesh, you can hug him and everything. It will be our Christmas treat. Christmas isn't far now."

"But mum, in English the word tomorrow means the exact next day. Your boukra has been stretching since before I finished year seven at school."

Yara closes the door of the bedroom they share in the small one-bedroom flat. She heads to the kitchenette to make food. Yara thinks about the Syrians she knows here. At first, they were all waiting, but after about five months, they started hearing back from the Home Office. Now it's just her.

Five-months-and-fifteen-days since submission date

Triiing-tra-tra-ta-ta-tam/Triiing-tra-tra-ta-ta-tam. Layla runs to grab Yara's phone when she hears the Skype ringing tone. She sets her father on the table.

"Daddy! Hello! can you hear me? Can you see me?

"The louder Layla's voice, the bigger Yara's smile grows. She watches her daughter tell Adel all of her school stories.

It's been five years since Yara last saw Adel in person. His face on the screen looks the same. The slow-internet-induced-pixelated-footage isn't flattering, but it definitely hides any ageing features. Yara hopes it does the same for her face at his end.

The years of studying and working two jobs have carved a million wrinkles around her eyes. Her back is developing a hunch, but she doesn't know how to stop it. If she could only afford to convert her dentistry degree to a British qualification, she would have more stability. Even enough money for a solicitor to get Adel a visa to London.

When Layla was four years old, Yara received a scholarship from a prestigious university. She took her daughter and travelled from Homs to London for what was supposed to be a one year's master's programme. It has now been over seven years since she completed her degree, and neither of them have returned.

Five-months-and-twenty-five days since submission date

They play 'Win the post!' to warm up the cold dark afternoon. Layla outruns her mother to the building entrance. She gets to open the letter if it has arrived. But, once more the mailbox is empty.

During the years of intense war, Yara never thought about going back to Syria. Even if she were to risk her and Layla's safety, legally they could not. They were no longer citizens. They owned no passports. Only travel documents. They are still refugees even after gaining indefinite leave to remain in the UK.

The only way to go back home and reunite with Adel is to become citizens of their new country. Yara has been growing tired of her life without him, of having to do everything in her and Layla's lives alone in a new country. The decision for them to be apart was the hardest of all. Adel had to stay with his elderly parents and had no visa to come. Yara recalls his words, "Layla deserves a normal childhood with no war, no noise and no death."

Six-months since submission date

Yara stalls on the way to the mailbox. She knows it is the last day of waiting and she knows Layla would love to open that letter. Layla thinks the same about her mother. When they realise they are both trying to run slower than each other, they pause and laugh out loud.

Holding hands, they walk to the mailbox. Yara fishes out the small key from her purse. She puts it in and opens the little lid of the box. Layla reaches in quickly and takes out the papers she finds.

A launderette advertisement. A two-for-one pizza voucher on collection only. A postcard from their friends Andy and Yvonne from their holiday in Spain.

That's it! No more post. No brown paper envelope with a government return address on it. Layla wraps her mother in her arms quickly. Yara feels her daughter's tears leaking onto her arms.

Six-months-and-three days since submission date

On her way to work, Yara calls the Home Office. A woman on the phone does not provide any details; she only says they will contact her by email.

Three hours later, at the bench in the lab, an email arrives saying: *'Your application is still in processing. Please do not contact us unless you do not hear from us within three months of this email.'*

Yara takes a deep breath. But she is betrayed by her tears. She has never cried at work. Not when her mother was killed. Not when her brother was forcibly "disappeared". Not when Adel was wounded by shrapnel. She never broke the rule. No crying outside her bathroom.

The caring-responsible-mother and loving-longing-wife takes the rest of the day off and goes home. She rereads the email, then throws her phone against the wall with all her might. It falls on the carpet and does not break.

Yara sits on the side of the bed, grabs her pillow and sobs into it. Three more months and maybe more with the chronic agony of waiting.

Triiing-tra-tra-ta-ta-tam/Triiing-tra-tra-ta-ta-tam. Yara struggles to get to her phone. She doesn't turn on the video.

"*Habibti,* please let me see your face. I couldn't get internet yesterday. When I finally got online and found no messages from you, I realised what must have happened. I know it's painful. I really know. But we've made it this far. We can wait a bit longer."

Adel's warm voice pours into Yara's ears like petals shed from a tree in a Spring breeze. Kind. Soft. Caressing her broken heart. Yara wants to tell Adel that he's right, they can do this. It is only few more months. Yet the seven-years-two-months-and-one-day since her asylum application all feel like rocks weighing her down.

"Right now, all I want is for the two-thousand-five-hundred-and-eighty-three miles between London and Homs to disappear. I just want to be held in your arms."

"I know *habibti*, I really know. I too wish I could be there holding you to my heart and never letting go again."

Yara always made sure not to break his heart with her tears but today she can't help but cry. They made it against all odds. No other couple she knows has survived such a long-distance marriage the way they did.

Thankfully, the call isn't disrupted. She turns on the video. They cry together. They talk it all through until they have a new plan.

Six-months-and-four-days since submission date

"Daddy! You're still online! Woohoo! I made it before electricity cuts," Layla says as she runs in after school.

"Hello sweetheart! Your mum and I were talking about how amazing it will be when you come in the summer. The weather will be perfect. You probably don't remember the lido where I used to take you swimming. They are re-building it. It should be up and running by July..."

"July! July is far away daddy!"

Adel reassures his little girl that summer will be here before she knows it and that Christmas in London will be fun. Yara smiles, nods and agrees with all he says.

There is no point in trusting the Home Office. There is no way she and Adel are going to put Layla through another disappointment after three months. Planning at least six months in advance is the right thing to do. If they hear back sooner, they will book immediately and surprise Layla. It's Adel's idea.

There will be no more waiting and no more 'Win the post!' games. Yara promised Adel yesterday to only check the mailbox twice a week -alone. Now they focus on reestablishing a routine and "normal life" like it used to be for the five years before applying for indefinite leave to remain. Work, school, homework, seeing friends and spending as much time as possible with Adel online in evenings and weekends.

"Normality, routine and fun are what Layla needs," Yara thinks, as she searches the best times to visit Winter Wonderland.

Ten-months-and-thirteen-days since submission date

Celebrating British Summer Time (BST) change has become a family tradition for Yara and Layla. Adel joins them online every year. They have a banquet of their favourite dishes, play music and dance. After the clocks go forward, the days start to feel a little more like Syrian days.

BST day is only five days away. Yara shops for the party food on the way back home. She's asked her neighbour to mind Layla for an hour at her place. But when she comes home, she finds the door already open.

"Layla! I told you never to stay home alone! Your key will be confiscated! Why didn't you wait for me at auntie Gertie?"

When Yara doesn't hear Layla's voice, she drops the bags at the door and rushes in. Layla is sitting on the floor. An envelope lies in front of her. Her eyes fixated on the envelope. Yara sits on the floor next to her.

Without a single word, Yara picks up the envelope and opens it. '*CITIZENSHIP INVITATION –APPLICATION FOR BRITISH CITIZENSHIP BY: Yara 14-May-1986 and Layla 13-July-2007. I am pleased to tell you that your citizenship application has been approved....*'

Finally, the waiting is over. Adel has been waiting. All of Homs has been waiting. They immediately videocall Adel. They celebrate. They laugh so much.

"First thing tomorrow morning, I shall ring the council to book the oath ceremony," Yara says to Adel. "Once that is done, we can apply for passports. *InshaAlla* God's willing, it's a matter of few weeks and we can come see you."

The virtual party has overrun. It's now nearly 9pm and they haven't had dinner yet. Yara is putting something together for them to eat, Layla turns on the small TV.

"*....From this evening, I must give the British people a very simple instruction. You MUST stay at home...*" declares the prime minister.

Yara emails the council to book the citizenship oath ceremony, right after the announcement. When she wakes up, she calls the council. No one answers. The email arrives few hours later. *'Due to Covid-19 lockdown, there are no citizenship ceremonies in the foreseeable future. Contact us again in a few weeks for update.'*

Yara feels numb as she reads the message.

Triiing-tra-tra-ta-ta-tam/Triiing-tra-tra-ta-ta-tam.

"*Habibati*, please stay safe. Do you have everything you need? We need to put a plan of how to go about this lockdown situation."

"Adel, they cancelled all oath ceremonies. We won't be fully naturalised until this pandemic situation is over."

"It's great we had planned a July trip then isn't it? All of Homs will be waiting for you to celebrate your return and Layla's thirteenth birthday!"

Yara and Layla nod quietly.

Adel tries again: "Think of it this way, for the first time you are ahead of all of the British people. You are already used to having a virtual life with me! Hahahahaa!"

Yara and Layla laugh along with Adel's slow-internet-induced-pixelated-footage face on the phone screen.

Dima Mekdad

Can you hear the people sing?

They dwell in strange rooms
the murky recesses of affordability
barely buildings, bedrooms with sinks
chair pushed up against the door
flakes of lives flung everywhere
a curtain, a quilt – who can really say?

A bare bulb hangs in an open window
no shade inside from day or night.
Still live go on; the rudimentary,
ramshackle, clutching at homeliness
the need for shelter unites us all
a hotel, a shed – who can really say?

In bleak electric heat, so many sing
It's a different song
all sing a different song.
Some higher, happier
some lower, more desperate than mine
flowing o through these days and nights
a verse, a chorus – who can really say?

The lawless, surging, movement of cars
the self-possessed trains below the buildings
so many pairs of eyes journeying on
the things they've seen, things they still see
those minds, all varied, wrapped in their own stories
a tragedy, a fairytale – who can really say?

/continued

Market stalls, street-sellers in threading gloves
the inside world spills out, a necessity
pavements become malls dressed in winter veils
motorbikes slip ghost-like in and out of sight
drunks stumble in high spirits from bar to bar
a wall, a urinal – who can really say?

In tall towers, in basement bunkers
so many singing their different songs
some sing of the joy of things
some sing only of the difficulty
the tunes flow through this city's veins
a love song, a death's lament – who can really say?

But can you?
Can you hear the people sing?
The miserable, the quietly ecstatic
can you hear the people sing?

Tom Alexander

UK LOCKDOWN BEGINS

Stay Lucky

"Stay lucky", John called as she pushed past him to the front door. "Take care of yourself out there."

'Yeah right, social distancing blah blah blah." Claire frowned. Fat lot he cared. Their third argument in two weeks stuck in the tiny studio flat. Over nothing really. But he hated being cooped up. They both did, and the news about coronavirus kept getting worse.

Standing outside their block she looked left and right. No neighbours in view. No police cars. Well, why shouldn't she go out? Everyone was entitled to one lot of outdoor exercise per day – with someone from their household. That last bit would spoil everything for her, even the dubious pleasure of heading down the High Street past a closed hairdressers and stacks of other closed shops.

There was a dead pigeon on the pavement by the kebab shop. Street-sweepers self-isolating? She hadn't seen a dead bird for ages. Sad really, the way it lay on its back with claws curled up like it had been trying to hang onto something just before it died.

Everywhere was so quiet. Window displays were missing, rows of dresses covered with thin cloths to keep them dust-free while the boutique owners hunkered down for a long wait. Longer anyway than the three weeks being talked about in Health Service broadcasts.

Claire quickened her pace, tried to turn her slouching walk into something more like healthy exercise. Not long till the next eight p.m. show of support for the NHS. When people were asked to open their doors and windows and clap or cheer. Last time someone even let off fireworks.

John had said it was stupid, that the nurses and doctors were too busy to notice. But Claire had stood at the window and felt less alone for a few minutes, less than she'd felt even before the virus made its appearance in the world's media and changed everything.

All this couldn't have come at a worse time for her and John. If they hadn't both had jobs to go to they might have broken up last autumn. But commuting, working hard and, she grinned, playing hard, had usually worn her out – enough so she could sleep. Probably John too, but with him sleeping on the sofa it was hard to be sure.

Claire went once around the council's big display of spring flowers and back past the kebab shop. She paused for a moment. The dead pigeon had disappeared. Probably the shop owner removed it. But what if it was a cat or a fox? Grisly to imagine what killed the bird was maybe infecting some other creature.

The streets were eerie, like a Sci Fi film about the end of the world. She did pass two blokes, made sure to social distance herself. Though with the rest of the High Street deserted she felt like a prat doing it. But rules were rules. Or guidelines. Whatever. She didn't want to catch the bug. Had been relieved when work told her to stay home. John's work too. If one of them had caught it…She'd seen a photo of a hospital in Italy, near where they'd had their last holiday. To think of anyone she cared about having to fight for each breath, waiting for one of those masks.

Briefly, John's face superimposed itself on her memory of the photo. She shivered, had to resist the urge to start running home. Remembered his kind warning as she'd stormed out, stay lucky.

Must get home. Make sure he's OK. Irrational maybe when she was the one outdoors, where the virus was lurking. But when had rational thinking anything to do with luck?

Camilla Reeve

Hopeful

My son's school's given us a plastic bag
filled with bread, potatoes, some pieces of fruit.
So far the news hasn't been too bad,

though it does seem things have gone a bit ragged:
we're stuck inside, the police been ordered to shoot
people driving to beauty spots. But the plastic bag

from our son's school was good. He's always mad
for bananas. His little brother's still cute.
The news hasn't been completely bad.

Mum's okay for instance, even with what she's had.
I'm just crossing fingers, hoping my grey suit
can stay at the back of the wardrobe in its plastic bag.

It's only likely to kill you if you've smoked fags,
I heard, and something about zinc, on the computer,
which is where most of my news is from. It's not all bad.

We're certainly not complaining, are all quite glad
of some potatoes, baked beans, a tin of tuna,
the loaf of medium-sliced white bread in its plastic bag.
And, so far, the news hasn't been too bad.

Jack Houston

The Fantastic Mr. Maj

Maj died on 28 March, five days after we went into lockdown. There was to be no body viewing at any time; they had already sealed and trussed him up proper, like he was some kind of toxic waste. Well, I suppose he was. He had COVID-19, you see.

His home-going was celebrated via Zoom, the government having just banned mass gatherings. Mourners logged in from disparate locations and we made for a pitiful virtual huddle. It felt like we had regressed to some kind of Soviet-y time-zone. It was strange anyway, but that such a social butterfly should be mourned via video was especially strange.

I use butterfly advisedly; Maj was a bright and exotic creature. The shona word for butterfly is shavi-shavi. It is farfalla in Corsican. In Filipino it is paruparu and labalaba in Yoruba. Every language seems to have captured something of the poetic and the ephemeral, the fragile and the exotic in the creature.

Here today, gone tomorrow.

'The time of the great tribulation has arrived,' the preacher delivering the homily thundered, his wobbly chin zooming in and out of focus on my phone screen. 'The four horsemen of the Apocalypse are riding. Blessed are they who die in the Lord.'

We were following proceedings from our home in Corby. It was a no-frills funeral; even singing was out of the question because the differences in broadband speeds made coordinating voices impossible. The preacher made up with an animated delivery, his arms swinging across the screen and all but knocking over his camera phone. I swiped on the phone to see if I could recognise the other mourners, making sure my hand was just out of shot. A few had disabled their videos so that only their avatars appeared. Others had their cameras positioned from under their chins which made them look like buddhas. One looked like she was in bed.

'But inspite everything, we Africans are like the Jews of John 11 v 19. We do not privatise grief. Our grief is a muscular and communal undertaking. We dress up. We make a song and dance of it. We gather, even if we may not have known the deceased that well. And always the communal breaking of bread. And, as you know, we circulate the plate for *chema* - 'tears' money because we frown upon those who go to an African funeral and eat and don't put anything in the plate in the same way that we frown upon witches. Because, you see, we are a village, even here in the diaspora. Yes, we are a comm.....'

The preacher stabbed something on his phone and it went on mute. He talked on because, his eyes being pinched shut in pious concentration, he was oblivious to our desperate gesticulations to unmute his phone.

'Nobody finds this weird?' my daughter Gugu asked, inflecting her tone at the end just like Barbie whom she watches relentlessly. She is nine going on nineteen.

'Hmm!' I said, not willing to incriminate myself and checking that I was on mute myself. It was weird yes. The whole thing was weird. A proper funeral is an important thing; it is a ritual as much for the family and community as it is for the dead. This was a poor substitute, but you don't say that in front of a child; they have a propensity of repeating things in front of the wrong audience. Like the time I said too much about the late Mr Maj in an unguarded moment and she repeated it at church.

'So dad, who is your bestest friend in the whole, wide world?' Gugu, the gingham-wearing, corkscrew-haired inquisitor, had asked, looking up from the luminous screen of her tablet. It was the night that the last Prime-Minister said the naughtiest thing she had ever done as a child was to run through a field of wheat. I wished we lived near large fields of wheat so Gugu could run through them every now and again and not make a sport of being a precocious wiseass.

'Hmm, let me see,' I scrunched my forehead for a while. 'I guess it's Mr. Maj.'

'The one from church?'

'Yes.'

'Oh the chubby one, right?'

'It's not polite to say people are chubby, Gugu, least of all those from church. I've told you off before for using that word, haven't I?'

'He is large though, isn't he daddy?'

'He is larger than most people, yes but it's not polite to say so, ok Gugu?'

'Ok, daddy,' she said, sounding unconvinced. She bent over her tablet.

'Dad,' she piped up a minute later, 'how comes the big people don't speak with Mr. Maj at all?'

Mr Maj was the oldest unmarried man at church and he dressed funny.

'I speak with him,' I said.

'Most of the big people don't though,' she doubled down.

'Maybe it's because he is a butterfly,' I said.

'Wait, what? What is a butterfly, daddy?'

'A butterfly is someone who goes to church but carries on....'

'Ahem!' my wife, who was sitting across the room and scrolling through her phone, cleared her throat loudly and glared at me.

‘Young lady, why don’t you find yourself a field of wheat to run in, or something?’ I said. She rolled her eyes and bent over her tablet. A few minutes passed.

‘Dad, why do you speak with Mr Maj in English though? Isn't he from Zimbabwe just like you?’ She piped up. Her Zimbabwe came out as 'Zim - bham - biwe' in sing-song, and she pronounced it with that amused turn of lip common among the too-white and too-young-to-be-troubled by black-consciousness.

‘Mr. Maj is Ndebele, my dear. Different tribe, you know, a bit like your Welsh mother in the UK kinda thing?’ I said.

‘So dad, you don't understand a word of his language even though you guys are from the same country?’ she tilted her head and looked at me through narrowed eyes.

‘No, Ndebele is actually very hard to master. Too many clicks, too much tongue rolling. Have you practiced your Mandarin today by the way?’

‘But didn't you guys learn each other's languages when you were growing up?’ she persisted. ‘Languages are easy to learn when you are little. Even Mandarin. I can now speak with Shan Li at school and my Mandarin is getting better all the time. And mum has been teaching me Welsh. *Bore da. Diolch yn fawr.* You could have done the same if you wanted to, after all Zim-bham-biwe is like a really small country, smaller than London, right?’

‘Right, Zimbabwe is a small country,’ I said resignedly. ‘But we just were never taught other languages, apart from ours and English.’

‘Why though, daddy?’

‘It's complicated.’

‘How..?’

‘Gugulethu, I need you to finish your Mandarin practice, ok? Shouldn’t you be more worried about your Shona anyway? It’s non-existent. It’s your heritage too, right?’

She rolled her eyes and looked down at her tablet. She looked up almost immediately.

'Dad, how come Mr. Maj is not married?' she asked.

On the night of the home-going service, Gugu asked if I knew Mr. Maj well.

'I knew him well, yes,' I said.

Matter of fact, I knew him from back home. When I met him again in England, he had settled in Kettering, not too far from where we lived. He acquired a council flat and a bulletproof Yardie accent in short order. And before long, he was running his own business, a small florist's.

'There have been three waves of arrivals to this country from Zim, bro,' he said when I visited, thrusting up three fingers in my face. His flat was a nice little number, done up in mauve and glitter throughout, on a busy road above a Londis. He set before me a platter of giant bratwursts, sourdough and cabbage soup and commanded me to eat up.

'A lot of people assume that the first large wave was when Mugabe began to murder Shonas for supporting the MDC. Not true bro; Mugabe was murdering us Ndebeles back in the 80s and we fled in our numbers, first to other parts of the country, but when that didn't work out so well, abroad. But we weren't the first wave either. The first was white Rhodesians just before and just after independence.'

I knew this of course but I allowed him to pontificate.

'The whites feared that Mugabe might be bad for the economy,' he said, deadpan.

'I guess the Shonas are just loud and they think that they discovered this asylum business,' I ventured, mid-chew.

'Damn right, bro. They think they invented the entire thing,' he said, othering Shonas as though I had stopped being one when I became his friend.

Maj was Ndebele. They are the largest minority tribe in Zimbabwe, and they nurse many grievances. The tribal prejudice against them was deeply-ingrained. We had a 'dissident' problem soon after the war, in the Matebeleland area where the Ndebeles live. President Mugabe sent in a militia and they were so efficiently ruthless the dissident problem never recurred, ever, but at a cost of twenty-thousand civilian lives.

'Collateral damage,' Mugabe boasted, waving a fist at western journalists. 'Africa needs a firm handle otherwise the gains of our independence will be reversed.'

It was in that milieu, when every Ndebele was seen as a dissident, or at the very least, a potential dissident, that I met the Mr Maj.

I had had no interaction with Ndebeles whatsoever until one sun-kissed summer, in which even the bees competed with us for shade under the luxuriant jacaranda and flamboyant trees, one came to our town and then to our church. His name was Chomi Mahlangu. He was a peripatetic artisan who made and sold brightly coloured artificial flowers. He fashioned them out of ladies' pulling socks, dipped in gaudy dyes and stretched over wire frames to create flamboyant multi-petal arrangements. His creations began to appear in the homes of our town, slowly at first and then more frequently as time went by and as the housewives who bought them gave them pride of place atop their display cabinets such that the others who saw them felt they were missing out on the latest trend, as housewives will always do, and bought them for their own living rooms to keep up.

Chomi was that type of person you know is not young but whose age you cannot quite deduce, camouflaged as it was by a slight build and a wardrobe of chintz shirts, bomber jackets, snug jeans and sunglasses which he wore even at dusk. When he pushed his sunglasses up into his spiky Afro, he revealed thick eyebrows and long eyelashes which fluttered, giving him an air of feminine sophistication.

'Ah, you look like that Lovemore Majaivana,' one of the young ladies remarked coquettishly. The resemblance alluded to was to a famous Ndebele singer and it was indeed remarkable. From the moment it was uttered, Chomi became Majaivana to all of us. But he hated his new nickname.

And he never married.

'Funny thing is,' Maj sat back like some potentate and licked his fingers, 'I flew to the UK on my real passport first time and they turned me back at Gatwick. I bought a fake passport and picked the name Majaivana and came back.'

He sipped on a large glass of red wine and patted his silk-shirted paunch.

'That name was my lucky charm. But the English people can't say Majaivana, bro. So it's been Maj ever since. His Maj,' he laughed and I laughed with him, marvelling at how much weight he had put on since I had last seen him in the old country.

I had not forgotten Majaivana in all these years, *firstly* because as I said, he was really the first Ndebele person that I came into contact with.

Our church practiced mass prayer during which everyone babbled at the top of their voices. When we grew tired and our voices subsided, *baba mfundisi* would take it up for a good while further in his ecclesiastical baritone. He would end with a benediction, in the name of 'the father, the son and the sacred spirit', his voice soaring to a crescendo and his arms splayed upwards. But when Majaivana came, we fell quiet and cocked our ears to hear Majaivana pray in siNdebele, his cadences and the dramatic power with which he delivered them as he bent over and beat his thighs with his open palms sounding like a drama recital. We understood none of the things he said but we liked to say to each other after church,

'Ah, did you hear mkoma Majaivana say – *'Tina zokudumisa unkulunkulu?'* while slapping our thighs with the palms of our hands just like he did and laughing as the exotic words rolled off our tongues.

Secondly, the man could sing. He had a falsetto and sang with tilted head resting in the palm of one hand, the other slung behind his back. It had a certain pathos.

Thirdly, Majaivana owned a car. In fact he was the only one who did in our church, that is to say, before he came no one did. And that car, unremarkable as it was, elevated him. The car was a brown Ford Anglia, the type with the bug eyes, the 'big grin' grille and a rear which slanted backwards like a hamerkop. It was a small car with two doors and the passengers needed to lift and shove the front seats forward to get into the back. Majaivana packed his flowers on the backseats and his passengers had to push them up and around their heads to ride in his car.

Invariably, the little Anglia needed to be pushed to get it started. Majaivana pushed it with us, us at the rear, him at the side shouting 'push, push' while leaning in through the open door to steer the wheel. Then, as the car gathered pace on a slope, he leapt in, slammed the door to and depressed and released the clutch in quick sequence. He had perfected the routine through repeated use. The Anglia always obliged; it would give a dry cough and splutter into life and zoom off. Majaivana carried a Gerry can of water in the boot for when the engine boiled over, which was often. And when he parked the car, he leapt out and extracted two bricks from under his seat and placed them carefully just behind the front wheels to stop the car from rolling away.

Fourthly, Majaivana invited me and my friend to sell his flowers when the school holiday came. We were unfamiliar with the concept of child labour; in any case if we had not been selling his flowers, we would have been in the small allotments which our families kept at the edge of town, digging and planting and pulling and burning and building mounds of earth for sweet potatoes. So we were flattered to be asked by this fine man who spoke our language in his own inimitable, a sing-song way.

But, while I got mine immediately, my friend Cosmas's father, a strict prison warden, took time to mull over whether to grant permission, as he might do if an inmate asked for permission to smoke.

'Something funny about that man, that Majaivana,' he said at last.

Eventually, he agreed that Cosmas could sell Majaivana's flowers, so long as we never went to his house.

'He brings the flowers here, you collect the flowers here and you drop the flowers here, he pays you here, understood?'

'Yes, sir,' we said.

On the first day, Majaivana gave us a selling tutorial.

'Don't allow the customers to finger or poke the stretched material. It will lose its tautness and sag. The flowers cost $7 each but if someone haggles, you can go down to $5,' he said. 'Commission is a dollar for each sale.'

Off we went, with our reds, blues, greens, purples, lilacs and whites draped around our necks and arms. We must have looked like butterflies.

We hit Cold Stream, a newly built residential township which still smelt of wet cement. We figured that people in new houses must have quite a bit of money lying about and be in want of decorations for their new homes. We kept to the main road, hurrying past houses whose wire gates bore signs which said 'Beware of the dog' and passing the church with the sign 'Little children, these are the end times' and where the women members wear berets and long dresses which reach from their necks to the floor.

'Boys, come by here,' a group of chattering women in doeks, sat under a grove of guava trees and shelling groundnuts, their legs spread out before them like logs, beckoned to us to enter their yard.

'How much?' they asked, fingering and poking the flowers.

'$7 only,' Cosmas responded hurriedly, his voice thickening and tremulous with the excitement of a possibility. 'But if you haggle, we can go down to $5.'

The ladies looked at each other and then burst out laughing. They bought a flower each at the princely sum of $5.

We made a tidy sum for Majaivana that summer. But he was run out of town at the end of that summer when tribal tensions boiled over across the country.

'Why did you call him the fantastic Mr. Maj?' I asked Gugu on the night of the homecoming.

'Because he was. He brought us flowers and chocolates. Plus, he dressed like nobody else,' she said, sounding a lot more serious than I have heard her. 'I will miss the fantastic Mr. Maj.'

'I will miss him too,' I said.

It was getting late and a breeze was gathering pace outside. I stood up to close the window and draw the blinds.

Taffy Nyawanza

The Postman

Normality arrives with the postman
The almost deserted street enlivened
By the arrival of his van, the quick confidence
As he opens the gate
Strides to the letterbox followed
By mail clattering on the floor

Doesn't matter what it is
Here's the outside world proving its existence
Whether a book
A postcard from a friend or a magazine

Proof this invisible hunter hasn't
Wiped out the everyday
Nor banished the bright promise of morning

The postman pushes the gate to and drives off
Red uniform in a red van

Vigorous superhero in league with Hermes
Delivering the magical and the mundane
Keeper of the seal of anticipation

Patric Cunnane

Front Doors

I met so many people
painting our first front door
but it wasn't just painting
it never is.
First chipping away rotten wood
and then an artful working of filler
to recreate the simple mouldings
a grey undercoat that smooths
before, finally
a loving coat of shiny navy blue.
It took all of a long day
on a very busy street
first the postman gave advice
then the guy delivering newspapers
to the shop three doors away
commented on how few women
paint front doors
our roofer stopped to say hello
and discuss the precarious roof
a new neighbour introduced themselves
complimented my work
offered friendship
finally my parents arrived
unexpectedly
and made tea.
I remember this, as I hide behind
another front door in another house.
We wipe its UPVC surface with alcohol
to remove virus, and
don't touch the mail until it's a day old
no live virus on it then.

This front door isn't elderly wood
but hidden steel within shiny white
when we lock it, nine bolts
shoot from its interior
into the strengthened frame.
In its centre a double glazed
stained glass window
made from a drawing of mine
a Red Kite wheeling in sky
looking for the windpath
my bird of prey guarding me.

Kim Whysall-Hammond

Hiding Myself

No straight promises
No straight love
No straight path
No straight art
There's no path in life
When walls block the way
You break through these walls
Scramble through the woods
When you find your path
You can understand
Only your passion leads you
In this cold rabbit hole

In these Covid-19 days when everyone must stay at home, I am staying in Leamington. Early in lockdown, I felt hot and cold all over because I caught the coronavirus. Fortunately, I was lucky enough to overcome it without developing heavy symptoms or requiring hospitalisation. Although weeks have passed, I still feel tired and sluggish.

It was a great shock for me to return to the real, hard-hearted world after peaceful Elan Valley, where I lived for two months in a happy dream with mindful self-compassion, and this shock later turned into a nightmare. It was very hard for me to understand how some people have a soul darker than a starless night. It makes me shudder to think of it. I feel my life is a graveyard of buried hopes.

I felt suicidal and I tried to cope with my emotional pain, frustration, and intense anger in a way that was harmful to me. Life became an agony, an utter agony.

I remember a sentence from Jane Eyre: "If all the world hated you and believed you wicked, while your own conscience approved of you and absolved you from guilt, you would not be without friends." I understood that I needed to be friends with myself before others. I read it again and again in English to stay in my mind and my heart.

Fortunately, during this process, I have been learning a lot about myself and how I have masked myself as an aspie woman.. For me, masking myself is more harmful even than not knowing I'm autistic. Masking means that I create a different Meltem to handle every situation. I have never felt a strong connection with my core which I never realised. When I am confronted with emotional upset, my brain immediately goes into "fix it" mode, searching for a way to make the other person feel better so I can also relieve my own distress.

In that period, I was very lucky to have Andy who loves, cares and believes in me, and I also feel thankful to my clinical psychologist, Dr. Rona Aldridge, from the Integrated Autism Service who met me every two weeks, and to Psychosexual therapist, Sally Duncan. I talked to her every week on WhatsApp. It's so painful but I think it's good to bring everything into the daylight and realise that nightmares aren't so scary separated out from the dark. Here in this process I will share what I have been learning about myself with you.

First of all, there was a question that has been in my head: how could I be more autistic every day, after every unexpected big emotional crisis? How was it that I was discovering new symptoms and that it was increasingly hard for me to control them at all? I know I can't be more autistic, so what is this drama? Am I pitying myself? Am I afraid of facing reality? Am I afraid of taking on my responsibilities? All the issues and self-doubt that affected me for years, I believed I had dealt with them, suddenly reappeared to haunt me, like ghosts. They overcame me.

I had been disguising my autistic self, the part of me I always hide. I'm struck with astonishment. When I stay my autistic self, my identity disappears in a dark rabbit hole… I can't reach it because I can't find it. I lost my identity with my masks… Which mask… Which identity… Myself… Autistic self.. Aspie self… My self?.. My?.. I... Down.. down...

Although I am 52 years old, I feel I have fallen down into a dark, cold rabbit hole. Age is no protector. I could easily hurt myself at any moment, I could easily be lost and cease to exist in this world. Meltem was gone. I couldn't reach her and her mind. Was it temporary? How and why was this happening? Why can't I control this anymore? How was it that I was so easily lost in a dark rabbit hole. I couldn't understand clearly and it was not easy to believe and cope with what I had been through, was going through now, whilst I was living in such a bewildered mindset.

Studies with women who can mask their autism very well, who are successful in their careers and diagnosed at an older age, like me, have shown that our masks can be destroyed in some cases in spite of ourselves.

In my experience, the cracking of the mask prevents me from controlling the situations that agitate my emotions and my senses as easily as I had done before and I have to face functional problems that I wasn't previously aware of… In a sense, I'm more fragile, more vulnerable and sometimes even unfamiliar with the process of adaptation which was very new and destabilising for me.

The situations that cause the cracking of masks could be: the menopause, negative emotions, big disappointments, unbearable stress, sleeping problems, life changes, relationship problems, traumatic experiences, communication problems, false accusations, intense sensory perceptions etc...

Looking back at the last several years of my life, I have been thrown into navigating most of the challenging aspects and life experiences mentioned above, and there has been a complete cracking of all masks. Perhaps this mask cracking process is still ongoing… This process is not easy at all, sometimes my soul, sometimes my heart, sometimes all my cells hurt, but it also causes me to recognise a liberation I have never known before.

The biggest benefit of this process is that I am learning again like a child to be open to re-evaluating everything with curiosity and enthusiasm. It also gives me the chance to reconstruct the rest of my life without hiding myself, without being subjugated to anyone and to live without fear.

Little by little
I came into this dark tunnel
Remembering disappointments
Remembering lies
Remembering past years
Like a song I forgot
I don't believe
How the story is set
A world full of hate
If you stumble no one will heed

Meltem Arikan

Day 83

My playboy tendencies now tamed,
I seek fresh air for its own sake
and head towards Finsbury Park.

We're like gigantic squirrels
who can't afford to sit still
and have to move on ceaselessly,

so I walk towards the pond
and bump into 'Max the Tennis',
who's cycling around

the deserted tennis court
as if around his dead child.
His mask is on his forehead

and mine below the nose,
yet we both feel as guilty
as some bank robbers,

both sharing a love
for nature and humankind.
This is the beginning of the end,

he says, breaching the silence,
his dark face turning darker.
Brexit blinded us

to the dangers of the virus,
is my unexpected reply.
His silence is poetry.

Hasan Kahya

Insomnia

I don't know if that sorcerer Odin
is working the sleep thorn against me

but when I lie down in the meadow
moon-dressed and bereft

the moon sails by and I lie
beneath its visions lapping and leaping

regular and irregular against the breast
bone beating in the ear fast and slow

while the beloved sleeps on unaware
in his steady sailing to a steady shore

that salt water is at it again
the meadow dying in its saline bath

and that goddess glides on
her tidal breathing sweeping towards Odin

Mary Powell

Coronavirus

I told my child
kids don't often catch it

what she took from this
was a nightmare
in which she caught
a spiky football
and tore her hands

In some desperation
I introduced
Fluffy Corry Mc Virus
at bedtime

We sit up straight
for Corry

receiving giant lessons
from this
tiniest of teachers

such as: needing time off
to think about
keeping the sky this lovely blue

Philip Burton

Something Wanting

In this land of a hundred Saints,
no want of one to adopt
this place, nicely far from
centre of town ,
centre of anything really:
Résidence de Sainte Madeleine,
Rue des Châtaigniers -
just fields grazing cattle
when last I came by.

The chestnuts are still there.
Dignified trees
which earn their keep
in one way or another,
with fruit and timber
for beams, wardrobes ,
palings, coffins,
affording shade, security
to the very end –
framing autumns and springs.

Plenty of space to turn and park,
walk a few yards,
adjust ones jacket and tie,
rehearse the necessary words
and what is best not said.

Relief that it's a sunny day,
that door is opened with a smile,
that carpet has a welcoming pile :

/continued

The auspices are good:
'Francoise is expecting you.'
Sounds like she's HERE today;
well, one has to smile,
n'est-ce pas? from time to time,
to prove that Time's not always
winning.

She's sitting near the window.
Net curtains gently shift:
silver-topped cane,
a sculptured head of hair,
most of her worldly goods,
and just a hint of a smile,
saying your name,
with stress in the unEnglish place
she always used.

Over the top!
The rest is easy going.
Today you do not think
to check your watch.
She pours the tea
made with the room's facility
for doing snacks and such,
and asks how people are,
though some are certainly
too far out of touch.

A head pops round the door
to check and smile and go.
Act 1 proceeds
without a single cue.

The House is still :
Today, no hoovers wailing
no muttering corridors.
It's Thursday afternoon.
Visitor Time!

Today is good;
no awkward waiting
for the curtain to come down,
seats to bang up.
Stage managers
and house staff
know their role.

At last the hour when
felicitations are due,
with kiss on cheek
and careful hug,
as two worlds
bid a fond farewell
that might become the last.
Outside, the car doors slam.
Cold engines burst to life.
Inside, the teacups rattle,
must be rinsed,
a chair replaced,
a window closed
before she feels the chill.

/continued

She rests a cushion
on the window sill,
looking at something
which is not out there,
but something
she can conjure still
from time to time:

Hens fussing round a yard;
turning the butter
fit to pat and pack;
grandfather clock
never quite sure of time;
keeping a glow inside the stove;
old walls, old door,
old table and her chair
to prompt the memory –
out there.
Out there, in a certain light,
at certain times –
beyond that
double glazing,
whiter than white!

Michael Tanner

The Flimsy

i.m. Florence Burberry 1925-2020. Died as a result of Coronavirus

It wasn't until your last day that I heard
of your flimsy, only heard the story of it
in what would be your final day with us.

Born a bastard you would tell people
those you knew and those you didn't.
Acquaintances, short-term carers,

taxi drivers, hospital staff who came and
went. No mention of a mother or father
on that piece of cheap paper, just a flimsy.

Martin Johns

Footnote: *Flimsy: Today the word is used to describe something that is weak or insufficient. The word originated from the paper certificate issued to a naval officer (like Flo's husband) when leaving an appointment to show as to their previous conduct. The paper was known as the flimsy. With the introduction of the Welfare State, illegitimate children were finally provided with birth certificates but not the same as for those who had their parents listed.*

Sleeping with C19

My sister lies awake for half each
night, staring at deepening darkness,
imagining the worst, worrying about
her children, our brother, and even me.
Her tiredness increases day by day
because at night she finds she cannot
sleep.

Such agonies of insomnia pass me by.
Having been to the gates of hell and back
in the company of this virus for the last
three weeks, I no longer need to fear,
can hardly stay awake, have no option
but meekly to obey my body's imperative,
and sleep.

Our brother in intensive care has now been deep
in medically-induced unconsciousness
for well over a week. He doesn't know
how ill he is, how soon he'd cease to be
if his ventilator was removed. But for now
he is alive, and stands a chance of being healed
in sleep.

Alwyn Marriage

708 today

That's fewer than yesterday
and the day before.
It sounds encouraging,
unless, of course, the 708th
was someone you loved.

My brother, for instance,
has for the last fortnight been
unconscious on a ventilator,
so in a way one might almost say
he died two weeks ago

except he didn't. He was still there,
cared for by skilled medical staff,
and from day to day, hope rose
and fell in us like the oxygen
being pumped in and out of his lungs.

He had a name, a history, was unique,
has been part of my identity
since the day that I was born.
This makes it all the harder now to accept
his new status as a national statistic.

Alwyn Marriage

It is the breath

It is the breath of opened lung that's listened for when we are hauled from dark
to greet the light.
It is the breath that shapes the words that welcome us,
that moves the love that folds us in,
the breath that ripples into laughter, falters to a cry,
swells need and joy.

It is the energy that drives the hand to shape, the legs to run, the mind to fly.
It is the warmth that draws together skin to skin, that consummates,
sustains the passage of the blood that feeds the heart.
It is the quieter breath that sinks us through the striving levels to tranquillity,
floats us to rest,
It is a spirit waking possibility outside the seen, the breath that stirs the curtain
at the edge of things.

It is the breath that's stolen by a secret thief, wrung to a thread
that leaves us gasping like a stranded catch within the fretted fabric
of a system crashed,
the breath that is a traitor to itself, an enemy within and out
that infiltrates security to turn us from each other and ourselves,
leave fearful eyes above a smothered mouth.

It is the breath of opened lung when we're first hauled from dark to greet the light
the breath we struggle to keep hold of in the final fight:

the last thing we let go when body slips to air and flight.

Helen Boyles

NATURE REPRIEVED

It was as if

We fled to the forest and the hills,
dug ditches, erected palisades, set
sentries at intervals around. And waited.

Messengers came with news of deaths
and from the temple, orders,
prognostications, warnings

about infiltration. Strangers we sent away.
We waited, looking sideways at each other,
fed ourselves as best we could.

Then we saw, as if we had new sight,
that dew was making brush strokes revealing
what we had overlooked: white blossom

of hornbeam and chestnut, the sky wiped
clear of mote and cloud. The land
filled with birdsong, larks and mewing kites.

For some this was world was new,
gilding their watchful stares with smiles
and startled revelation.

For us it was an older world returned,
the backdrop to our childhood's careless
pass through. Now we walked more

slowly, attending and exploring,
the air tense with fret and wonder,
almost a time of innocence returned.

Frank McMahon

Wild flowers on May Day

Glad to be out in the freshest of air
with clear sky in spring, salted
by the wind from the sea, she followed
an old lane not much used and began
to search among wild flowers that leant
under hedgerows. She found flowers
she had never noticed before.
They appeared suddenly on my phone,
image after image, bright, fresh.
The wild into my hands.

She showed me bluebells for constancy
with sorrel for affection, honesty's sincerity,
valerian for strength, snowbell for the blood,
greater stitchwort property of pixies,
fern for humility and some magic too.
Young beech leaves, green for energy flow,
milkmaid for hope in sad times,
red campion to guard against loneliness
and bring in the faeries' blessing.
Taken by my daughter, the flowers shone together.

Rose Cook

Going Wild

They have taken to the streets. Wild animals
have begun to take advantage of cities in slumber.
Jackals howl in Hayarkon Park, Tel Aviv.

The timid have come out into the open,
a racoon steals across a deserted Central Park,
goats and sheep graze near Istanbul airport.

In Japan, sika deer stroll over a pedestrian crossing,
don't worry, they're doing just fine.
Outside a shuttered shop a sea lion waits

in Mar de Plata, Buenos Aires and fallow deer
meet up in Harold Hill, London.
Grey langurs, monkey about, their tails

questioning what's happening in Ahmedabad, India.
While in Ajaccio, Corsica, a wild boar nibbles
a long lazy lunch in a neighbourhood garden.

Shaggy horses graze outside a stadium that's
seen better days in Srinagar, Kashmir, and dogs
rest a while on a deserted road in New Delhi.

Horned goats parade in file through Llandudno
in Wales, as sea birds mimic gondolas in Venice.
For all of them, no lockdown, freedom to roam.

Martin Johns

The Return

Venetian gondoliers are silent, the canals are as glass
reflecting swans and dolphins as a leash of deer
catch the sun on a front lawn in Essex.
Hark! The goats of Llandudno
have formed a choir – a top tenor bleats and eats
a hedge into shape for the return of tourists.
The tourists are replaced by sheep at Istanbul airport

Day's hindrance seeps into twilight's privilege.
The watchman of Kerala is an elephant.
Fearless jackals howl their harmonies
across a Tel Aviv park and the raccoons
play hide with no one to seek them
in central New York.

By the grace of dark's silence,
I unfold my redundant wallet.
Little brown moths that cannot raise a tune
from plastic notes, on the advice of an owls'
parliament, dance away from the acrylic world
in search of night stock.

Sue Johns

At Ashton Court, Clifton

I walked on the grass
In warm sunshine among trees
Traffic sounded far away
Beyond the blue hills and
The shape of buildings, tall
Towers and everywhere cluster
Of aerials and people huddling
For news of the dead and dying
But I had eyes only for each
Tremulous blade of grass
Proud among cowslips
I said to each you will survive
You will inherit the stars
The earth and all that lies between
And I said the same to the orchid
Who was prouder and wore
Its blue and purple blazon
Without any green wings

Michael Baron

Thinking with the Hand

The hand is the window to the mind
so said Kant.
I sit and write by my window,
thoughts gushing like a waterfall,
words toppling over into a whirlpool.

I sat and wrote a lot
at the beginning of Lockdown,
by the lounge window
looking down to the eerily quiet street below.

I soon got used to the peace and quiet,
spotting the odd neighbour and dog walker.
I still felt part of the world
viewing from that first floor window,
before I went out more.

A German phrase *Denken mit der Hand* –
thinking with the hand,
feels like the right thing to do.
I find solace with pencil and notebook,
thoughts coming and going like a meditation.

As I let my hand wander across the page,
the pool of words settles
into a quiet stillness, peaceful.
I want this feeling to go on.

Jenny Messer

A Journey Around My Flat

Descending the snowy mounds
of my bedclothes, I encounter
the vast plains of the living room
which, after a weary traversing
lead me to the kitchen,
where a cup of chai masala
transports me to exotic India,
as does the leftover rice
encrusted on a dish.
Now a feline, emerging from the undergrowth
of a chair, reminds me of the dangers and glories
of the African veld.
Weary from my travels, I yearn
for my snowbound eyrie, but must first traverse
the bathroom, where a splendid waterfall
causes me to give grateful thanks
for the wonders of nature.
Strengthened by my adventures
I now am able to climb and reach my goal,
and take a well-deserved rest.

Fay Lipshitz

Socrates awaiting

How to describe the scent of a spring raging with colours
That is impossible.
How many impossibilities are here...
Socrates saddened
Looking at the closed circle of the quarantine.

Anna Maria Mickiewicz

To the Quarantine

I lift my eyes to the clear sky
Its blue colour is now limpid and pure.
Like a miracle in front of my eyes
A little bird sings to a possible future

I put on my special mask
Afterwards I go out for a short walk
I need to buy something in a shop
I step away from the human ghosts

At home, my husband works while I cook
The best meals we enjoyed ever
Thanks to the quarantine we are in a honeymoon
Full of harmony and paradise love full for ever

I know some people died and that are bad news
But animals and plants are reviving mostly
And a green future will be the consolation
In any place and at every nation

Maria Cristina Azcona

Walking Our Allotted Span – Colehill, Dorset

When did I know who you really were?

By the purply-blue periwinkles, you glimpsed
early on our walk from home,
creeping amongst the hedgerows
in traffic-free Colehill Lane?

By the stitch-worts, close-by, whose white petals,
you read, gather force before
exploding like fireworks in summer,
scattering seed and light?

By the old oaks, where we turned left,
fresh-dressed in lime-green leaves;
you said take they take years to live and die,
I wondered when this plague would end?

In the open meadow, then, where
new grass-tips bristled like paint brushes
and, before I could blink, you lay down
as if entering a warm bath? Yes.

It's there I knew - in another life,
you were a sylph, a sprite, a nymph,
so nimbly did you move from air to earth,
so grounded in that soft, green moment.

And it's there I felt peace again.
Before we headed home, walking
our allotted span together, calmly,
the other world dipped in darkness.

Tony Horitz

Gardening in lockdown

I shouldn't call myself a gardener – possibly a junior
groundsman or someone still on work experience.
My wife's the real deal, taking cuttings, nurturing
seedlings, potting on, pruning expertly – she's even
propagated a Tree Peony from a single leaf.

I still struggle, I'm ashamed to say, with annuals,
perennials and the endless Latin names. I'm happier
with the destructive side of things, the mattocking
and slashing, but during lockdown I've discovered
something that I hadn't known about before –

that gardening can be quite like playing Patience,
in which a turn of card can free a run of moves.
Each garden task may open up the next.
So, clearing an unruly patch of nettles, brambles
and creeping honey-suckle (I checked for nests) –

which had been on my mind for far too long –
suddenly fed into another plan: to fill up
gaps in the straggling hedge we share with neighbours,
to create a visual barrier to help with social distancing,
which we're in danger of forgetting if we chat.

When I've filled the hedge with brash, I have
a second small illumination, realising that
the cleared ground could be hoed and raked,
ready for wildflower seeds – another long-term
dream of ours. First I need to deal with roots.

I dig down to the nettle's weed wide web with its
criss-cross of supple yellow cables. Pulling one,

I watch energy rushing through the ground
like a gunpowder trail in a silent movie. Now I'm
ripping it like dodgy wiring out of crumbling plaster.

Sometimes a metre's length comes up, with nexuses
like junction boxes linking a whole colony. The soil
fragments. It's halfway to a tilth. I add the roots
to the hedge, where some may thrive – as with Patience,
winning's sweeter when opponents aren't defeated.

This Thursday we'll applaud our NHS, whose staff
wouldn't have to be so brave if properly supported,
funded and equipped. I'll clang my spade and fork
because our next task is – to quote my darling wife –
turfing those slimeballs out of government.

Mark Haworth-Booth

Coming Down

Aubretia blurs the capstones
of the high retaining wall.
Beyond is the bluest sky
ever to grace a Pennine hospital.

The virus has returned me
to forebears who could draw
upon visions. Fever has baked
bricks for walling-up doors

crying out to be sealed:
air miles must reduce to inches,
gardens must adopt the fields,
profits must be ploughed back in.

The world has straightened
its clothes, is prepared to be
the cloud-wide courtyard
sprung with pools and reflective smiles.

I get up and walk my dream
like a leper not yet believing
a virus can be any sort of Saviour.
But in closing, I begin to sing.

Philip Burton

Social Distancing of Sparrows

for Anne

There's none.

They dive-bomb the birdbath
in chittering brawls,
ambush the hedgerows
like cacophonous children
sent home from school.

Happier than Hitchcocks,
they shriek blue murder
rustling curtains of beech;
are merry, masked raiders
of our lurching, lost ark,
our world on hold:

Theirs now.

Helen Pizzey

LOSING TRACK OF TIME

Half-living through Lockdown

I have no plans
and I'm empty of thought,

then I suddenly ponder –

is this like those hours
before that final breath
when good memories blur,
and dark scars fade?

That thought leads me on

to the time we'll leave the warm
or cold heart of our homes;
worries and hurts never mended
will cease,
no more potholes to fall through.

Now thoughts flood in –

Please may there be that radiant light
some speak of –
a new dawn to kill darkness.

I pray there will be family
and kindly people – sun, rain,
mist, snow, moss, flowers, trees
and the trickle of running water,
frogs, bees, birds, tigers and elephants
oh and … … …

Val Tigwell

Arsenic and Pearls

Locked down, Isolated,
denied the Sacraments.
Told I am vulnerable,
treated like a child
who must do 'this'
must not do 'that'.

I have lost all sense of being 'me'.
Offered to be looked after,
but I don't want any of them.
They want me to conform;
the 'me' that I am has never totally
conformed - acted as ordered.

Somehow, treating me kindly
makes it worse - suspicious.
Getting control gently
speaks of subterfuge and spying.
'Shuffle off' they are saying,
'you're not needed any more
the world can do without you.'

Can it ? Don't I add that little extra,
that twist of lemon, that acid drop ?
I have a few more pearls to cast
before the swine, the herd.
A few more arsenical bonne mots,
Before I shuffle off - in my own time.

Jane Sherwin

All these weeks

lock down in the vein of a cow
who has lost her calf

a wardrobe looming
big dark and empty

the dangerous lorry driver
who gave me a lift long ago

this heat sweltering and stormy
then unexpected cold nights

pyjamas sloppy clothes no shoes
mostly just bare feet

a big oak door with an iron handle
that closes quietly behind me

Kate B Hall

A New Way of Living

Do you stand among the trees and grasses
breathing in the air
they have cleansed
– because you can?

Do you listen to the birds
singing to you
because you have chosen to stand among
them hearing their voices?

Or do you check the clock and sigh
with frustration
because every day is so much time
to be filled?

Have you lost the art
of being in your own space
and filling the hours
with thanks
because you are still here
surrounded by life?

Tina Morris

Lockdown: Easter Sunday

4am: awake again.
How long have I lain like this?
Every night for two weeks now:
chasing, facing up to bad dreams trapped in the web
of sleep.
Too tangled, too deep to fully understand.
Anxiety winding a tight band around my skull;
tossing and turning before I succumb,
and finally sleep again.

8am: lie in bed.
Switch on the radio: the latest news.
The same politicians, excusing bad decisions;
met with derision by angry nursing staff.
Are these fools having a laugh? Where is our promised
PPE?
Bereaved parents, siblings, friends, weeping, heavy-
hearted:
never mind where this all started, where will it end?
Over the bodies of a million dead?

12pm: can't go to town,
so I go to town on the garden instead:
weed the overgrown flowerbed, rip ivy from abandoned
roses.
The unseasonal sun burns my nose; thorns shred my arms.
My lovely garden has lost its charm. Now it's a prison.
Yes, Christ may have risen; Christians rejoice!
But I'm locked up here in this green tomb:
that's the stark choice.

4pm: boredom strikes.
I try to write a poem, start a sketch,
stretch myself to write my long-awaited novel.
Instead I end up grovelling before the empty screen.
How do you motivate yourself when all you feel is fear?
When everything you hold dear disappears?
Beloved family far, far away:
the stone in my chest, still there, on the third day.

8pm: Face Time:
hard work over for the day, grab a shower,
wash away the gardening grime, slap some makeup on.
Who would have thought a mobile phone
could bring such joy into our home?
I'm not alone at all, the proof is here to see:
my family, laughing, clinking glasses, toasting me,
safe and sound, across the Irish Sea.

12am: Back to bed,
no need to dread the coming night.
No need to fight dark thoughts: comfort reading soothes
my brain.
Pages of well-crafted words contain the seeds of hope:
my tired body slithers down the slope of sleep.
Away beyond my bedroom window, in the black-deep,
the moon still shines, bright stars twinkle,
I content myself with thinking: all this will pass.

4am: Awake again …

Margaret Whittock

The Ghost Inside

For Mental Health Awareness Week 18.5.20-24.5.20

Why do the footsteps follow me,
The icy breath, the sinewed hand,
Clutching so close I can't be free,
Freezing my will to understand?

This land is where the spectres loom,
The desert of the dry-bone mind.
No sunrise to an endless gloom,
No comfort here of any kind.

In deep troughs of introspection
The will to walk has walked away,
Speech, though voiceless screams rejection,
All plans and hopes have had their day.

On distant pathways signs of life,
Like shapeless figures in a mist,
Begin to sharpen like a knife
In thoughts and dreams of all that's missed

For now a half-life lingers on
Fed and cared for, prescribed pills.
Catatonic oblivion
Hides the hellish war of wills

George Wright

During the time of Corona

"Butche...i" he says. He stopped as he was walking past. He repeats, "Butche...i" The Gestalt app in my brain springs into action. It goes for closure of gaps, joins the dots. "Butchery?" I ask, emerging from my reading. A confused brain app quickly scans the street. I already know. No butchers on this street. "There are other shops..." thinking he was new to the area, new out of "lockdown." The words barely leave my mouth. "No no... Bu-cc-e...i!" He emphasises the sounds for me. I focus as the trundling of the red buses, three going one way four coming the other, create gaps in my hearing. I visualise a possible spelling. He stands on the other side of my small table. Metal. Round. One of those classic French/Italian outdoor cafe tables. Cream. Innocuous. Accompanied with the atmospheric hues of *joie de vivre* and intellectual cultural discussions. Vodka mini-bottle in one hand, he gently repeats. "Oh! Bucce...i..." pointing at his earplugs. "Ohh!" he repeats deeply, narrowing his eyes pointing to his mobile phone held in the other hand attached to his ear with a wire, "... he is singing!" I smile watching the ecstatic look in his eyes, half closed. "Operatic..." he informs me in between. "Buccer...i" "Ave Maria...ohhh!" he repeats touching his heart, the fingers moving as lightly as butterfly wings, gentle tapping gestures. "Ahh!" he breaths out, eyes still slightly ajar. The head tilted upwards catching the late sun rays on his forehead. He is in Heaven. And of course he thinks I am Italian. I wait for an innocent fragment of silence. "I like Ave Maria..." I say, trying not to intercept his ascent to the Heavens riding on Bucce..i's voice. "He is..." his finger holding the mini-vodka bottle moves across his eyes. A bitter twist of the lips... "...but ohhh!" he repeats. I understand. *Bucce..i is blind but what a voice*! Slowly the brain begins to deposit small fragments of memory for my perusal... On one of the BBC3 concert broadcasts I had heard an opera singer; "blind" was mentioned by the presenter at the end. Radio BBC 3, my new-found salvation from the shit adverts on Radio 4 and the repetitive mouthing of the ugly, brutal, robotic voice of the incompetent arrogance of the Bo-Jo the Bodger and his GANG's pronouncements, ordering us about, constantly infantilising us...I escaped. So Radio3 broadcasted the opera singer, singing Ave Maria. Schubert. I tell the man holding the sacred blessed water, the mini vodka in one hand, lost in the Heavens that I had heard him on BBC3. No reaction. Just an imperceptible nod. He is not impressed. The buses are also playing havoc with his hearing, I think. I wait. "What?" he asks suddenly, shaking himself out of Heaven. "Radio 3." I repeat. He takes his earplug out. Smiles, "I am an old man," he says, "I can't hear that well..." My turn to smile at the man who is likely to be much younger than me, lost in his music. "I know Bucce..." I say as another two buses trundle past one way barely two meters from the end of the pavement where I have found refuge for my daily espresso; they are like tanks. The loud double clunk made by the two loose cast-iron manhole-covers as the buses go over them echoes in the chambers of our brains...all conversations severed. I notice he smiles. Happy that he has managed to share his love of the music and the singer with someone, a stranger, on the street. He leaves a trace of a smile as he disappears beyond the Italian tricolore heavy canvas awning hanging down from the top of the shop front, delineating the borders between the adjacent shops. Or is it a new Corona-inspired protection screen?

The possibility of chance encounters on this pavement in front of Antonio's grocery/deli and to share tiny morsels of life with complete strangers has become a lifesaver. People with whom I would not otherwise share anything. There are no concerts and even so they may be too formal too tainted with snobbery, elitism, upper-classicism, knowledge of music or being incorporated into pretending that you do, discussing the "mechanics" rather than the spirit or emotion it provokes...that's not "knowledge" of music...it is showing off by brandishing "knowledge" of the "history" and "technicality" of the music. My advice to myself, hold onto the spirit!

It seems incarceration, of being forced to lock ourselves up, as though we are responsible for causing the death of thousands including frontline staff or that the NHS will be saved by our staying at home rather than good management, cash injection, supply of PPEs, as though we are the ones who decimated it over the last ten years... as though we are guilty for being alive at a time of deaths!

Forced into silence. You cannot criticise. This is a war. We are in it together, let's get through it first…bullshit! With which opposition politicians colluded. Just like under any dictatorship. To be stripped of logic or any rational, critical thinking. To be forced into solitary confinement or familial confinement. Take care of number one, as your motto! To be prevented from showing compassion, care, dignity, communality...to be forced to think of fellow human beings as your enemy, their sole purpose to infect you. Kill you. To strip you of your humanity. The insidious brainwashing so total, it leaves us breathless. We are incorporated into policing each other, from standing in queues, to sitting in our gardens, to the number of toilet rolls we buy. And where to stand in a shop or walk on a pavement... and much much more madness, anxiety and stress creating situations! The fact that scientists of the Independent SAGE are adamant that 55,000 deaths could have been prevented in the UK, actually England...shocks and creates rage! It is quickly replaced by gibberish in ministerial announcements! No one wants to or even cares to wrap their heads around the "facts"; we now inhabit a fact/truth free world. How could this happen in Britain, a cradle of democracy, freedom, best national health care in the world, the best education, centre of the Arts, fifth richest country in the world, with the highest levels of poverty, children suffering from malnutrition and largest numbers sleeping on the streets? The land of unashamed lies. The levels of "I am not responsible" and just "moving on" by the Bo-Jo the Bodger and GANG, has left deep scars and has traumatised citizens.

My table is piled up with snippets of numbers. From across the world. I wanted to know the death tolls. Of the world. Of the countries I had travelled to along my life. I am a witness. And I don't want to pretend that I don't see, that I don't feel the pain, that I was not there. Every night I search for the evidence of the murders. Sometimes I analyse them. Sometimes I record. At times I am obsessed with writing them down. Random clusters of countries with numbers...

June 21, 2020 - US 120,000 - Brazil 50,000 - UK 43,000 but(65,000 in fact- 8,100,000 world infections- 444,000 world deaths- May 8, 2020- Italy 30,000-UK 32,000-July 23, 2020-4,000,000 infected- 143,800 deaths-France 30,200 deaths- South Africa 6,000-World 15,000,000-July 28, 2020- UK 46,000- July 30, 2020-US 150,000-India 30,000- Brazil 91,000- Unemployed: US 39m-UK 3m-South America 37.7m

At times in shock but not acknowledging it, faced with the ease with which the numbers are piling up! Just piling up...How quickly all sense of "normality" slipped through our fingers, minds, souls... How easily we were being cajoled into adopting the "new normal" to accept absurdity as normal...

I keep finding fragments. Numbers, thoughts scribbled on pieces of paper. Scattered on my table.

5.8 million people who share this world with me, on my birthday, today, have been infected with Covid-19. I am not part of those statistics yet. I haven't been tested. The test kit arrived two days ago. I'll do the swab and send it the following day...a stupidly complicated way of trying to get this test done. So obviously clear that they are not keen to provide testing.

359,000 people of this world died of the virus in the last five months, extinguished - while I became a Covid-19 "veteran," as the ruling elites have declared "war", or a survivor. I suppose both words encompass nearly the same meaning - if I am keen to avoid the militarisation of the pandemic caused by a virus, I would lean towards the word, "survivor"! And I am still not part of the statistics just like thousands of others. The ruling elites need low numbers...I wrote on May 29, 2020.

Figures continue to float across everything I see. And the faces of those killed float above them.

Two days after my day of birth, on May 31, Trafalgar Square is throbbing against the centuries old pervasive injustice of extrajudicial murders. *I can't breathe* becomes the voice for us all. We witnessed his slow choking under the knee of a policeman. Minneapolis, USA. But it happened in front of our eyes. Four days before my day of birth.

June 3, 2020 thousands turned up across the world. Threats were brandished by the impotent ruling elites, especially by the GANG at Number 10. We will be arrested for violating the Corona rules. We should not hit the streets.

We did throughout the UK and across the world, in our thousands!

I can't breathe - the slogan faces me in front of the Lewisham Police Station as the number 75 bus crawls past. Around a thousand mainly young people fill the public space, reclaiming it. Buses honk. Cars honk. Repeatedly. Applause rises. Cheers. Raised fists of solidarity thrust out of car windows in response to those raised on the pavement. The killings in the US find a mirror in the deep frustration and anger against incarceration and the deletion of the future of the youth. They have been robbed of their tomorrows. Now what?

A police woman walks by, black. Amongst a very mixed group with their homemade cardboard slogans. A chorus of *I can't breathe* rises in the company of loud clapping and cheering. The uniforms respectfully and cautiously stand against the wall of the brand new police station behind us, of what used to be Cheeseman's the department store. No "presence" of police or policing. A hands off approach. Double-decker busses crawl slowly blasting their horns and the echo bounces between the surrounding buildings. A Palestinian flag by the road side – flutters...a reminder of the apartheid murders and suffocation of a whole people. Two guys swagger past wearing facemasks. Loud *No justice – No peace!* accompanies their swagger. Was I like them, these young people? Half a century ago. They make me smile. We go down on one knee. I share in this knee-down. It has become an effective symbol of opposition of rebellion when other forms of expression are silenced. Gagged! When people pay with their lives...June 5, 2020.

I continue to be inspired by James Baldwin who I read in the 1980s. "I am history. History is now. I chose to be an optimist. White people invented the Nigger." – film, *I am not your Negro.* And I am a witness just as he was.

In the time of the Corona, Antonio places a round chocolate sweet next to my coffee cup on the saucer...with a smile! His usual 'cheeky' smile although I am aware it may hide much. Will he survive the pandemic, will his customers come back, will he be able to keep his five assistants, two Eritrean/Italian young women? He reads my questioning eyes. "My mother made it," he says, "it has a tiny bit of raspberry in it." The proximity of the thumb and forefinger brought close to his face indicates the amount of raspberry. I thank him. His three-way conversation in Italian continues. About football! My sign language, about the price of the sweet, is blocked. "It's on me," he says touching his chest. He takes my £1 with a smile. For the espresso. The football players discussion is uninterrupted in this process – the hands make the espresso, put the choco sweet on the saucer, the £1 coin is taken, the octaves of voices go up and down and everywhere else, the till is rung, coin thrown in. "They just buy the boys train them for a while they begin to bring in spectators money to the club..." a brief silence then the anger, "... then they sell them, they SELL the boys for millions! They don't care!" comes the final full stop blast from Antonio with his hand slicing the air. The other two momentarily speechless. "I agree," I say as I pick up my piping-hot espresso cup, specially heated up as I like it hot and head for the door.

Although the noise of buses, increased numbers, the diesel noise and pollution is becoming overpowering and unbearable on this road of two-way traffic for busses at times lined up at the traffic lights further down the road creating a red tall wall reminding me of the Berlin wall I first experienced in 1971 is getting over the top, where at times I can't hear the person talking to me, I continue to come. During the Corona lock down, I came on my bike at times, for what felt like scavenging or foraging for food at the four stalls that remained in the once busy open market. And not much of a choice. I cooked what I found rather than what I wanted. No plans for a menu. It was part of learning to live without making plans for tomorrow let alone beyond. A liberating sensation. For a woman used to working to tight schedules...And I savour the streets, the air, freedom. After my four stall stroll I would head to Antonio's; he did take-away espresso. In time, they allowed me to sit on one of the fold-up metal chairs leaning against the wall; it was forbidden to put them out on the pavement. I made a table using one of the empty boxes piled up in front of the shop. I sat surrounded by empty cardboard boxes from Italy. Hardly anyone on the street, very few buses, no cars, hardly anyone around. It became my oasis during the time of the Corona. Where escapees came to shop desperately seeking a bit of humanity and Italy.

Footnote: *The blind opera singer was Andrea Boccelli...*

Aydin Mehmet Ali

Making Marmalade in 2020

Halving grapefruit, oranges and lemons,
then squeezing out the juice, removing
pips and pith, fiddly but quicker than what comes next.
Eyes locked on peel, each thin slice a chalk mark
on a prison wall as the future slows.
Strive for harmony: sugar and the wake-up call
of citrus. Sample, more reaming, squeezing.
Boil for this long, says the book but history
tells you different. Time stretches out
until it starts to flake and wrinkle,
the setting point when it's time to pour
into the cooling jars, twist and seal each lid.
Store until the moment of release,
beyond your prediction or control.

Frank McMahon

Blue

You awaken,
eyes focusing
as reality slowly seeps in,
obscuring the night's dreams.

Another day – what day?
Monday? Is that why you feel blue?

Blue like the summer sky
outside these walls.

Blue like the toenail
you stubbed three weeks ago.

Or was it four?

Blue like the leaflet posted
through your front door.

Wash your hands!

Blue like the wallpaper
on the stairs you descend
as you migrate south;
your commute to another day

in lockdown.

A.V Shepherd

Night's Midpoint

Why fear when there
is nothing to be seen?
This unseen is a killer.

These days come
and go
like shadows in twilight.

A comforting blanket
of sameness, leisure, peace.
All falsehoods.

Here, at night's midpoint
my heartbeat falters loudly,
fills my head.

Death slips softly into my soul,
across hot night air
fear strangles my tears.

I hear the susurration
of those struggling to breathe
all over this night.

Kim Whysall-Hammond

Last Days

All is not well in my world.
This room is my room
and not my room.

The house that is our home,
is on stilts
and walking away from me.

I see a bumblebee,
take a sip of nectar
and fall to the earth with a thud.

The wind blows and thunders,
then bursts
into dry sobs.

The children of my heart,
are nowhere.
Not a sound.

My lover is at a loss
and walking
through the walls.

Our small dog who dances
lies down
and dwindles.

All the world is one
warning sign and I cry,
where in the world are you?

Mary Powell

UK LOCKDOWN ENDS

Lockdown VI

Soon,
our gates will be opened
and we shall emerge
onto our streets
like caged birds will,
when allowed to fly again,
rediscover the sky.
But we will soar with caution,
knowing we are ready-made prey
for an invisible predator,
oscillating among us.
Corona is still here
and there is no certainty
whether soon enough
we are not ordered back
into our cages
until our predator creeps away.

Joseph Kaifala

I said No

What surprised me was,
when they said I could go out
I didn't want to.
My world has become this,
my home, my house,
complete as a child's
made vast by imagination
streaming the world,
wild and all the time,
my beloved here too.

I am afraid that to go out
will break all that,
make my world small again.
Seems ambition has gone
leaving me unconcerned.
I notice how I like to laugh.

Rose Cook

Emerging: 2020

The sprouting shoot, still sheltering within the seed,
even as the root reaches down into the soil,
questing for the water, that will feed the sudden rush
into the bright sunlight of coming days.
This is the way of enforced solitude, waiting for the sign
to thrive
and burst forward into the world, unfurling tendrils,
spreading leaves and hardening stems,
to thrust up towards the sunlight of a glorious existence,
free to bend into the wind and breathe
and breathe
and softly, slowly, celebrate this life.

Nick Alldridge

The Best Things In Life Are Free

A young girl is dancing in an empty aisle
She twirls, drops a shoulder, lopes
drops a shoulder, turns, mouths words
The Best Things In Life Are Free

There's the courtly dance of the pandemic –
my turn or yours by the bananas –
and a young girl dancing free

Socially distanced behind her,
pinned in the queue, see through her swooping lens
over buy one get nothing free. Words, words, words

Better not speak. Let ministers and advisors
emerge through doors for the daily briefing
to socially distanced foxtrot or waltz

Whatever the best things in life are
she finds dancing in an empty aisle
the best things in life are free

Barbara Saunders

The Bicycle Shed

The Bike Shelter's roof's in despair;
        rain seeps in but there's been no teen in there!
                the hut is subdued, derelict and neglected,
                        every one of the Fifth Form cyclists
have deflected.
The Bicycle Shed was the hub –
        the pupils with wheels' cosy club,
                an age-old rite of way,
                                a shining bright ray,
                                        for knowledge-thirsty
adolescents –
                                                heralding
their route to pubescence.
The Cycle Hub's canopy's sprung a leak,
        and the long grass behind's reached its peak,
                the forlorn edifice mourns each ecstatic
young pair,
                        trysts of love-smitten teens, longing
for their first dare.
The wind blows some news-print – the shed's now aware,
        a virulent stalker warns all youth beware,
                no more would the young, fertile, e'er
propagate,
                        years of two-metre distancing
henceforth is their fate.

Loraine Saacks

My May 2020 Diary Excerpts and Ruminations

Living room table 11.55 pm 6 May
Bottle, bottle burning bright,
in the middle of the night -
vinegar and box of pills…
Oh what is it for?
To cure all our ills?
These are on our table sprightly,
I'm sometimes using
these rhyming words frightfully!

Patio 9 May
10.10 am: Bluebottle on patio…
glowing green blue of body
but for many, and me at times
an odious creature…

Forlorn closed sun umbrella on
texture of frosted glass table -
bluebottle still on ground 10.27…
airing its wings,
or wounded?

There's a lonely ant, and
a gold yellow glittering
fly hovering over
the paving stones, momentarily…

/continued

And the bluebottle can
fly thank goodness,
but only temporarily
it seems…

Patio from window 15 May, early morning
A piercing cry…
A high-pitched scream…
a screech of
yellow and lime green
amoeba dagger-like leaves and
cherry pink pearl blossoms -
a background to a
solid closed
grey, but yellow "sheened"
sun umbrella sombrero…
solid and calming as a
wary Britain gets
back in step with
the outside world...

Fryent Country Park,
Brent, 25 May
Yesterday…
all my fantasies seemed
so far away…

When all at once
I saw a host -
a host of shining
buttercups, a shimmering
of pale pink thin bulrush-
like weeds, and
exquisitely pinkish-violet
clover, all
tremulous in the frail,
kind wind, but part of the
intensive fields of
Fryent Country Park…

There were “distancing” or
“isolating” couples
within this particular
Spring of 2020, in
discreet scenes
of love...

Rosemary Wolfson

Summer Solstice

and day dilates to the sun's stretch
across space. Tentative, above our heads
clouds sculpt the blue.
Here on the station platform, thinly spread and separate
we are globed in our protective pods,
mouths muffled, eyes downcast.
Just the dog beside its mistress is content,
eyes bright, oblivious to all that circles its security.

A mother, son beside her, silent, masked
meets eyes, shares knowledge of support, dependencies,
the need to hold the wind from others following.
Inside we shrink in doubt, subdued by powerlessness:
What plans are being hatched, decisions made unknown
to us?
Can we re-board the train, will it take us where we want
to go?
And do we know where that might be?

You briefly shared our refuge, shared anxieties.
Resourceful, capable, you still forged links online,
recruited teams, built structures to resist a building storm.
We interwove reflections on the seashore after swimming
out
to shed our heaviness.

But now, on the platform, ready to depart:
'I'd like to know when I can go dancing again!'
Trailing empty carriages, a few blurred faces through
the pane,
the train draws up: time to embark.
We part, wave, cannot hug.

The train pulls off.
In our minds we try to balance sickness, health,
fear, happiness; we measure caution against risk,
know we must look up, stretch to the sun
before the dark curve of the turning year folds in,
remind ourselves that it must tip again towards the light.

Helen Boyles

Dream

I wake up from
a difficult dream
and find out
there is no disease.
No one has died.
My friend who nursed me
in prison
has not been ill
for the last six months.

Life goes on
except after years
of suffocation
under grey smoke
the sky is blue
in Tehran again.

Nasrin Parvaz

From March to Now

Then
the air's stillness of an evening
had the full sound
of a thick covering.

We lay quiet in bed,
and pulled down our black blindfolds
to keep out the light. You said

who came before put this
and this into the garden,
the small pot, the iron trivet.

Even the apple tree
messaging the world
with its green icons.

Now
the evening makes
a different kind of sound.
No wind but the *thunk thunk*
of the Blenheim Oranges.

Everything prepares to come again.
Even sound is the same
through time.

Gill Horitz

The Ghosts of Lockdown

Ghosts come in the night and deal with my household rubbish;
another set of ghosts, by day, handles my garden refuse.
Others again spirit away my recyclables; today they dropped
a tin can which slid across the street with a sound
like rolling thunder in the all-enveloping stillness.
Down in the village in the local pharmacy
a ghost keeps paracetamol under the counter
and averts the gaze beneath her mask
from the lame and the halt distancing themselves
from each other, and from her.
Out at sea there are rocking boats full to the gunwales
with ghosts of a different extraction, fearful ghosts,
terrified ghosts who have no idea of what they might find
if they ever make landfall; but what, really, are their chances
in the mist, with blue men climbing over the rotting sides?
I imagine crowds of ghosts. They're on the tenth floor
of high-rise city blocks, angry ghosts, frustrated ghosts,

hungry ghosts with wailing children and no access to the parks,
to the air and sky which surround them but bring no help,
only a reminder of what has been lost.
Each night on TV I see ghosts floating through
the ICUs gently tending other ghosts, some of whom
may never come back to life; there is an intense lack of sound
from machines which should have been bleeping
but have now gone long beyond that.
We are left to reckon with their stillness,
registers of another death, another ghosting as families
still wait, with hope and without hope,
as the toll climbs, as the long-expected equipment
again (and with a new litany of excuses) fails to arrive.

/continued

And there are warehouses full of ghosts, endlessly
picking, sorting, responding to our outrageous orders -
for books, videos, printer cartridges, whatever goods
we might deem essential, but are not on the government list
that dictates what is corporeal, what is ghostly.
Where will all these ghosts go after lockdown? Will they have
their own care homes, where they will be allowed to rest in peace?
Or will they continue to haunt us once life is restored to
what passes for normalcy, reminders as the deaths climb
of all that we don't know and about which we have not cared?

David Punter

FURTHER AHEAD

Something new

They'll want a say in how some things should happen,
like, for example, how you wash your hands:
things you will notice that occur quite often.

The air has dangers for a citizen,
as when a virus or a spore just lands.
They'll want a say in how some things should happen

and COVER UP will be a daily slogan
against new hazards no one understands.
Things you will notice that occur quite often

official experts analyse and liken
to harms with unknown names from distant lands.
They'll want a say in how some things should happen,

even some customs people held in common,
for centuries, vanish as new fear expands –
things you will notice that occur quite often,

like how to speak, to look, to greet and even
to eat and drink come under new commands.
They'll want a say in how some things should happen –
things you will notice that occur quite often.

Mark Haworth-Booth

Author's Footnote: *This was written in response to Ebola in 2015.*

in order for us to take off successfully according to the will of all those who have clearly stated that they wish to fly to the moon it will be necessary for us to have complete control of the spacecraft because the voyage simply will not be possible if every passenger is at liberty to grab the controls and start flicking switches as and when it pleases them and therefore anyone who agrees to share in this great adventure must also agree to certain precepts namely that the pilot has complete authority to guide us to our destination but now there are some who say that they reserve the right to see how the pilot gets on with the job and if he does not perform to their satisfaction then they reserve the right to grab the controls after which heaven knows what chaos may ensue so it is imperative that we recall the great example of henry viii who if he found a person an encumbrance extirpated them and it is in that proud historical spirit the retention of which is exactly the kind of national tradition for which we have been fighting for so long and so ardently that I would wish any passenger to take their seat which incidentally will be fairly uncomfortable in order to test the sincerity of those who say they wish to participate in this unique enterprise and when we reach The Cave On The Moon it will be a simple matter to turn it into an exploration base because this chasm which is thirty miles long and 100 metres wide is structurally sound and its rocks contain ice and water deposits which can be turned into fuel beneath the Marius Hills on the near side a lava tube created by volcanic activity about 3.5 billion years ago it would protect all committed passengers and their equipment from extremes of heat and cold as well as radiation from the sun's ultra-violet rays although no-one has been inside it or scanned it but committed persons are confident it could provide us with just the opportunity we are looking for to create a safe space and secure our future outside the planet although faint-hearted earthers say they are wondering if there really is water or ice in those rocks and demand to know how they could be turned into fuel which if it was possible how expensive it would be when we know it can be done economically because china russia india and the us have expressed an interest in the cave so we shall have to be quick and the japanese who discovered it have already claimed priority but we are certain there is room for all and this beautiful cave could offer many fruitful opportunities for international co-operation and above all trade

Josh Ekroy

Lockdown or LOCKED IN?

In all this enforced space
and silence,
have we learned anything
about our selves
or are we chanting
the same old mantras
in well-practiced idiom?

To grow, our thoughts
need to suggest, subliminally,
what our hearts
are desperately conveying
-allowing our silences
to curve into the heart

in order to move on
and joyfully, up,
into the light of truth

Tina Morris

Laughing behind a Mask

Sweaty rooms, fire hazard full, the audience is excited, drunk, breathing in each other's faces. The comedian on stage is inches from the front row and the laughter rebounds off the ceiling and walls building a crescendo to rip the roof off. None of this can be socially distanced.

Unlike music or theatre, proximity and intimacy is an essential component of stand-up comedy. Ditsy open mics, clubs with dodgy wiring, sleek purpose made clubs that fill their rooms with office parties.

When these cramped gigs were abandoned and Edinburgh Fringe put to sleep for a year, the entrepreneurial stand ups valiantly embraced online gigs and outside connection, even masked audiences in socially distanced spaces. But virtual experience can't recreate the live sense of being in the presence of a great comic. There is no zoom delay, the timing of a joke is all. As it is, most comedy has been watered down to online sketches and vlogs or delayed zoom meetups that bring a different flavour to the set ups and punchlines. You can't ask a comic to repeat the joke. Stand-up comedy has its own engine, a rolling laughter that builds like a wave and the comedian is a surfer riding with it.

People will say that it's ok, that they are creating new spaces and new ways of working but the fact is you need to hear other people laughing for it to work. Any dips in the mood create a void that creeps open wider and wider as internally the audience begins to agree 'this isn't funny'. The belief and trust that the comic is funny is half the battle. They are repeating back to you their facilitation of your laughter. A magician pulling back and revealing the surprising truth that creates that reaction. Laughter is infectious, a virus and to catch it you need to be close. So what is the future for this evolving lifeform? How can it be recreated? Finding connection through laughter is more important now than ever.

There is hope at the end of this tunnel. There is more opportunity and hunger for comedy now than there has ever been. Podcasts are thriving, online series are given more viewing than any television sitcoms and live performance will return, just in a distanced cabaret style seats and behind masks.

But we need laughter, we need to hear it and see others smiling. The masks are there but they aren't stopping us. The internet is a playground of connection that could turn the comedy world from a hierarchical boys club into a network of difference, embracing everyone and anyone who dares to switch on their camera or talk into their phone to the audience.

Perhaps the sweaty armpit above a pub clubs will struggle to return, but the new generation of comedy is global, fluid and all encompassing. The only criteria for a stand-up performance is a mic an amp and a dedicated space to perform all of which you can get on your laptop, phone or tablet. The future of comedy is democratic and more open now than ever before, so perhaps the answer is not to mourn the loss of the night shift gigs but to enjoy the creativity this new era is ushering in.

Rachel Sambrooks

Sometimes I can't hold up the wreckage

falling into disrepair
as I pursue the fantasy
of making a difference in the world
that might change the shape of fate
while we watch we watch
societies hurtling towards dismemberment
rather than mapping out alternative paths
but we are not Joseph filling the storehouses
against inevitable famine running down natural resources
and we strip the cupboards of our health systems bare
decide against fuelling the minds of children
                                        facing our despair
following the lead of The Irresponsible complaining
yet too few or fragile to know what else to do -
I do not know what else to do.

Simon Lichman

Lockdown was easy – but what next?

My wife and I, in our mid-70s and in health best described as robust fragility courtesy of previous interventions and preventive medication, were eased early into lockdown by a suspected contact, which turned out to be a false alarm. So Lockdown Day found us already isolated, with a couple of supermarket delivery slots booked, the local convenience store offering to pop round with essentials, and younger and fitter friends and neighbours offering to fetch and carry. The following week brought a card through the door introducing us to a local volunteer who has cheerfully collected prescriptions, posted parcels that would not fit into our local pillar box, and ventured into the supermarket jungle when deliveries failed us during the "slot drought". A few more local shops quickly set up delivery services, so we were well served.

We were lucky. So lucky. With each other, a roof over our heads, pensions that had for years kept us in frugal plenty, a small garden, and the exercise bike recommended by a cardiac nurse, we were very conscious of the plight of those with more onerous responsibilities and lacking our comforts and facilities. Survivor guilt set in. What could we, should we do? Friends and family, remote but in daily contact, assured us that the – at that time – simple instruction to stay at home, protect the NHS and save lives was all that mattered.

So, we stayed at home, built a raised bed in the garden for vegetables, set up online groups to keep in touch with painting, sewing and musical friends, and enlivened the Thursday evening applause for the NHS with music at the front gate, waving across the road to neighbours and to the firefighters and paramedics who would drive gratefully by with lights and sirens.

That, for us, was the easy bit. We knew that lockdown could not continue forever. We were fairly sure that there would be further waves of infection, for which the rules could not be so black and white, and we became fearful. We recalled the hapless residents of EM Forster's underground cities in *The Machine Stops*, forced into a devastated outside world when their infrastructure collapses. We empathised with Byron's captive in *The Prisoner of Chillon* who, unjustly imprisoned, becomes reconciled, institutionalised, even develops a touch of Stockholm Syndrome and eventually regains his freedom "with a sigh".

So what to do? Certain things are clear. Music in groups is unlikely for the foreseeable future. So is supporting our (until recently) Premier League football team. Equally, despite strenuous efforts, our local theatres will struggle to perform in a space safe for both players and audience. On the other hand, we have been assured that our local deliveries will continue. We are going with the flow and, still feeling rather guilty, leaving others to worry about supporting the vulnerable, raising enough tax, and making the buses and the railways viable.

When we are the "last ones standing", when we are called to the colours, just as a desperate government raised the conscription age limit in 1918 ... then we shall go to the Front as loyal virus fodder.

Richard Reid

Making a World One's Home

The soul selects her own society,
surrounds herself with truth and beauty –

garlands of exquisite memories
that wear their fragrance like gods and lovers

lost in an unimaginable shower
of grace, alight with the unbearable

pleasure of being here, steadying me
with the thought that whatever happens,

nothing is forever. Everything changes
when one has lived a long time alone.

Whether we appreciate it or not,
we do not own the fruits of our actions.

We are separate from our actions
as a decanter from the wine sparkling in it.

If we accept the world as a gift,
not take the gifts of the world for granted,

we may still learn to cherish what we have,
be thankful for everything we never had.

Notes to lines quoted: *'The Soul selects her own Society' is by Emily Dickinson and 'when one has lived a long time alone' is by Galway Kinnell.*

Shanta Acharya

Prayer

Grant us the wisdom to survive –
like trees that live long, enriching the planet;
loyal protectors of the realm, standing firm,
asking nothing in return of heaven or earth.

Grant us the wisdom to imagine –
the need to give and forgive, not merely receive,
like an oyster transforming grit into pearl,
the giving growing, becoming something precious.

Grant us the wisdom to rejoice –
a long time after we are returned to earth, the lives
we leave behind may cherish the fruits of our action:
a million species saved from extinction.

Grant us the wisdom to love –
love without limit, love that casts a widening
circle of light for the world to walk forward in,
singing the songs of its forgotten springs.

Grant us the wisdom to pray –
strive to set right the injustices we perpetuate,
courage to change the things that must be changed,
else there will be nothing left to live for.

Shanta Acharya

REFERENCE

Pages where Authors' work appears

First Name	Surname	On pages
Shanta	Acharya	7, 135, 136
Tom	Alexander	35
Aydin Mehmet	Ali	97
Nick	Alldridge	112
Ata	Alsady	11
Meltem	Arikan	54
Maria Cristina	Azcona	81
Michael	Baron	77
Helen	Boyles	68, 118
Philip	Burton	60,86
Steve	Champion	16
Rose	Cook	74,111
Patric	Cunnane	51
Josh	Ekroy	127
Michelle	Fuller	14
Kate B	Hall	92
Mark	Haworth-Booth	84,126
Gill	Horitz	121
Tony	Horitz	82
Jack	Houston	40
Martin	Johns	65, 75
Sue	Johns	76
Hasan	Kahya	58
Joseph	Kaifala	8,110
Yan	Li	4,6
Simon	Lichman	132
Fay	Lipshitz	79

Alwyn	Marriage	66, 67
Frank	McMahon	10, 72, 105
Dima	Mekdad	28
Jenny	Messer	78
Anna Maria	Mickiewicz	80
Tina	Morris	93,129
Taffy	Nyawanza	41
Nasrin	Parvaz	120
Helen	Pizzey	87
Mary	Powell	59, 108
Sue	Proffitt	22
David	Punter	122
Liba	Ravindran	25
Camilla	Reeve	38
Richard	Reid	133
Loraine	Saacks	114
Rachel	Sambrooks	130
Barbara	Saunders	113
A V	Shepherd	106
Jane	Sherwin	91
Michael	Tanner	61
Valerie	Tigwell	90
Margaret	Whittock	94
Kim	Whysall-Hammond	52, 107
Rosemary	Wolfson	115
Sholeh	Wolpé	26
George	Wright	96

Author Biographies

Shanta Acharya DPhil (Oxon) is the author of twelve books. Her publications range from poetry, literary criticism and fiction to finance. Her recent books include *Imagine: New and Selected Poems* (HarperCollins, 2017) and *What Survives Is The Singing* (Indigo Dreams, 2020). Founder of *Poetry in the House*, she hosted a series of monthly poetry readings at Lauderdale House, London, from 1996-2015. She served twice on the board of trustees of The Poetry Society, UK. www.shantaacharya.com

Aydin Mehmet Ali was born in undivided Nicosia. She lives between Cyprus (North and South) and London, where she sought refuge from war; an unaccompanied minor. An intellectual activist, writer, translator, educationalist, traveller and cyclists, she set up and managed numerous projects focusing on women and young people. A renowned anti-racist and anti-militarist. Her work appeared in many international anthologies, journals, magazines, performed across the world, taught at universities. Books: *Turkish Cypriot Identity in Literature (ed./translator)*, *Pink Butterflies/Bize Dair* (short stories/poems), *Turkish Speaking Communities & education - no delight (academic)*, *Forbidden Zones* (short story collection), Nicosia beyond barriers... (anthology; co-editor/project coordinator). *Intellectual Fragments* interrupted by Corona, 2020. Director/Founder of Literary Agency Cyprus.

Nick Alldridge is a South London poet who has recently been working mostly on poems connected to myths and legends, particularly poems inspired by the Finnish epic The Kalevala. His collection of more personal poetry, connected to themes of health and recovery – *Playing With The Pieces* – was published by Palewell Press in 2016.

Ata Alsady has Dutch nationality and lives in London. She is a cellist and has published *Birds* - a collection of poetry in free Haiku style.

Meltem Arikan is a Turkish author and playwright. Arikan has written 11 books and 5 plays. She was short-listed for the Freedom of Expression Award in 2014 by Index on Censorship for her play 'Mi Minor' which the Turkish authorities claimed was a rehearsal for the

Gezi Park demonstrations in 2013. Their subsequent hate campaign, fuelled by state sponsored media, forced her to leave Turkey to start living in Wales. In 2019 Turkish court accepted Gezi Indictment seeking life sentences for 16 people including her.

María Cristina Azcona lives and was born in Buenos Aires city, Argentina. Psychopedagogist and Family counsellor. Bilingual writer. She has written 30 books, published in Argentina, India and the US. She is President and Founder of the Worldwide Peace Organization (WWPO) and the International Forum for Literature and Culture of Peace in Latin America (Paz IFLAC).

Michael Baron has had poems published in *Other Poetry, South Bank Poetry, The Journal, The Third Way, Jewish Quarterly, Herne Hill Society, Letterpress Poets Anthology, Morley College Magazine, World Haiku Review*, and several poetry websites He is editor/co-editor of: *On A Bats Wing, The Night Shift* (Five Leaves Press), *The Cockermouth Poets: 1700-2012* (River Poets (2010) Cockermouth), *How Hall: Selected Poems of Tom Rawling 1916-1996* (Lamplugh Heritage Society), and *Wordsworth and the Famous Lorton Yew Tree* (Lorton Historical Society). He was awarded an MBE in 1980 for services to autism.

Helen Boyles has always found poetry the strongest, most effective voice for expressing experience and responses to events like the present Covid-19 challenge. She's an active participant in poetry events and is Co-chair of the Devon-based creative writing group of Moor Poets. In recent years Helen has had two poetry collections: *Catching Light* and *Transitions* published by Indigo Dreams. Another collection is forthcoming from Palewell Press during 2021.

Philip Burton has been a Lancashire head teacher and a poetry practitioner for children. In 2019 he concurrently held four poetry competition First prizes, including Sandwich (Kent) Poet of the Year. Philip was recently awarded a Commendation in the 2020 Poetry Society Stanza competition. His poetry publications include *The Raven's Diary* (joe publish 1998), *Couples* (Clitheroe Books Press 2008), *His Usual Theft,* (Indigo Dreams Press 2017) and Palewell Press will be publishing *Gaia Warnings* in 2021.

Steve Champion is an incarcerated writer whose most recent book, co-authored with Craig Ross, *The Architect: How to Transform Yourself and Your World*, was published by Palewell Press, 2019. You can find a video about the writers and the book at https://www.youtube.com/watch?v=mduPQiZfo-I

Rose Cook is well-known in the South-West, having read in many venues and festivals. A published poet, her work has been shared through literary magazines and performance. Her latest collections of poems are *Sightings* and *Shedding Feathers,* both Hen Run publications from Grey Hen Press. www.rosecook.wordpress.com, rosecook108@gmail.com

Patric Cunnane's latest collection, *The Ghost of Franz Kafka* is published by Palewell Press. www.palewellpress.co.uk. He co-organises readings by Dodo Modern Poets in London and elsewhere in the UK and Ireland. https://dodomodernpoets.wordpress.com. Patric lives in Folkestone and also writes fiction and drama. In June he read for the first time at Au Chat Noir (The Black Cat) in Paris. In November he won first prize in the Folkestone Writers' short story competition. patric.poet@zen.co.uk. Tel: 01303 243868

Josh Ekroy lives in London. His collection, *Ways To Build A Roadblock*, which mostly consists of C21st war poems, is published by Nine Arches Press. His work has appeared in *Best of British Poetry* (Salt) and *The Forward Anthology. The Cave on the Moon* won third prize in the Tongues and Grooves Prose Poem Competition 2018.

Michelle Fuller lives in the UK and formerly worked in the NHS for nine years. Having experienced the UK immigration 'hostile environment', she uses her creative works to raise awareness of the system's injustices. *Tales of a Hostile Kingdom*, an animation based on her writing, depicting the hostile environment, was produced by Refugee Journalism Project. https://www.refugeejournalismproject.org/2019/11/01/tales-of-a-hostile-kingdom-2/

Kate B Hall, born 1945, writes poetry, haiku, reviews and fiction. She has published two haiku collections *Running for Nothing* and *Irises.*

Her poetry collection *The Story is* and her new pamphlet coming out in 2021, both published by Bad Betty Press. Kate recently completed a Creative Writing MA and is now working on her next Haiku and poetry collections, and struggling with a collection of short stories and a 1/3 written novel!

Mark Haworth-Booth was born in Yorkshire in 1944. He studied English Literature at Cambridge University and Art History at Edinburgh University. He served as a curator at the Victoria and Albert Museum 1970-2004 and has written widely on the visual arts. Mark lives with his wife in North Devon and is an activist with the Green Party and Extinction Rebellion. He has published two books of poems.

Gill Horitz has worked in the Arts for many years with various organisations and communities, developing community theatre and creative projects, including programming literature and running writing groups. She attends a regular poetry group in Dorset, led by Paul Hyland. Her poetry has been published in magazines and anthologies. Her first pamphlet, *All The Different Darknesses*, was published in 2019 by Cinnamon Press.

Tony Horitz has been writing poetry for many years, alongside a career in community theatre, educational drama and theatre in education. Two of his plays were published by Samuel French Ltd and a collection of poems, *Voyages*, by Word and Action (Dorset). He is a member of Poetry in Progress, a group of seven Dorset poets, convened by Paul Hyland, who meet regularly to share new work in Blandford.

Jack Houston is a writer from London and is poet-in-residence at Hackney Libraries. His work has been published widely, including in *Blackbox Manifold*, *Magma*, *Poetry London*, *The Rialto* and *Stand* magazines, and has been shortlisted for the Basil Bunting, Keats-Shelley and Brick Lane Bookshop Short Story Prizes and the 2020 BBC National Short Story Award.

Martin Johns has a long track record of publication in poetry magazines and anthologies. He has given readings including at the Poetry Café in London, and with Carol Ann-Duffy at the Manchester

Royal Exchange. Martin has collaborated with several composers with words and music performed in Manchester, Leeds and Northamptonshire. He has an MA in Creative Writing from Manchester Metropolitan University. His pamphlet *Resting Place* was published by Palewell Press in 2019.

Sue Johns originates from Cornwall where she started performing as a punk poet. She has published 2 pamphlets and 2 full collections, the most recent being *Hush* (Morgan's Eye Press 2011) and *Rented, Poems on Prostitution and Dependency* (Palewell Press, 2018). Her work has appeared in a wide range of anthologies and magazines including *Poetry News, The Morning Star, Southbank Poetry, Prole, Brittle Star, The Atlanta Review* and *The Big Issue.* Sue is currently studying for an MA in Writing Poetry.

Hasan Kahya was born in Limassol, Cyprus, and has been living in London since 1972. He works as a translator. Hasan's poems have appeared in various Turkish, Cypriot, and British magazines / anthologies. His translations of 49 poems from Fikret Demirag were published in 2015, titled *In a Silence that is God's Music.* His own poetry book, *Two Rivers*, followed in 2018. His latest collection, *The Pale Map*, will soon be published by Exiled Writers' Ink.

Joseph Kaifala is a Sierra Leonean writer, philosopher and lawyer. He is the founder of the Jeneba Project - providing educational opportunities to adolescent girls in Sierra Leone. He is currently the Principal of the Center for Memory and Reparations - facilitating remembrance and common narratives around the Sierra Leonean civil war.

Yan Li is a poet and journalist. Now living in London, he left China in 1988. A member of *Dodo Modern Poets* and *Merton Poets,* Yan in recent years writes in English while most of his work is in Chinese. His recent journalistic writing in Chinese includes: *8pm Thursday: Clap for NHS Doctors, Nurses and Carers* and *100-Year-Old Army Veteran Captain Moore: It's You Who Are Truly Great.*

Simon Lichman, was born in London (1951) and has lived in Jerusalem since 1971. He has a B.A. in English Literature from the Hebrew University of Jerusalem, Israel, and a Ph.D. in Folklore from the University of Pennsylvania, U.S.A. He has been a university lecturer and is the Founding Director of the *Centre for Creativity in Education and Cultural Heritage*, which brings together Israeli and Palestinian communities. His poetry appears in journals and his own collection, *Snatched Days*.

Fay Lipshitz was born and grew up in South Africa. In 1973 she emigrated to Israel, where she has lived ever since, in Jerusalem. She trained as a librarian at the University of Cape Town and worked at that profession until retirement. Her creative activities consist of drawing and printmaking, and writing poetry. Her artwork has been exhibited in Israel and abroad, and her poems have appeared in several collections.

Alwyn Marriage's eleven books include poetry, fiction and non-fiction; she is widely published in magazines, anthologies and on-line, and has won several competitions. Formerly a university philosophy lecturer and chief executive of two literacy and literature NGOs, she is currently managing editor of Oversteps Books and a research fellow at Surrey University. She gives regular poetry readings and workshops in Britain and in many other countries around the world. Her latest poetry collections are *Pandora's Pandemic* and *In the image: portraits of mediaeval women* and her latest novel is *The Elder Race*. http://www.marriages.me.uk/alwyn/

Frank McMahon lives in Cirencester. Published poet: *At the Storm's Edge* published in January 2020 by Palewell Press; also on-line and in print. Podcasts with Ragged Foils Productions: *Detach from World*; long poem *Family Gathering*. Play broadcast on local radio, *A Death in Flanders* 2018. Working on a children's novel, plays for radio, short stories and poetry.

Dima Mekdad is a Syrian Londoner. She is the co-founder of Qisetna: Talking Syria, a cultural project which focuses on using storytelling as a tool for personal empowerment and social engagement for Syrians across the globe. Dima wears several hats, among them a storyteller and a new writer. She is interested in the human experience and is particularly curious about connection, belonging, healing and growth.

Jenny Messer was born by the sea and now lives by the Thames, water being a source of inspiration. She was a Picture Researcher at the *Radio Times* and a photographer's agent. She loves to create pictures with her poetry. She began writing sixteen years ago after a brain injury but has been an avid reader since childhood.

Anna Maria Mickiewicz is a Polish-born poet, writer and editor who writes both in Polish and in English. Anna moved to California, and then to London, where she has lived for many years. She edits the magazine *The Literary Memoir*, and *Contemporary Writers of Poland* (USA). She is a member of English Pen. Her first collection of verse was published in 1985. *London Manuscript,* published by Poetry Space, Bristol in 2014 and *The Mystery of Time,* published by Flutter Press, USA 2019. http://faleliterackie.com

Tina Morris has had seven poetry collections published, including one co-authored with photographer T.K. Metcalf. *The Visitors* was published by Calder & Boyars in *New Writers 7.* Her writing has also appeared in many anthologies including *Children of Albion* (Penguin), *Doves for the 70s (*Corgi*), New British Poetry* (BB Bks), *Poetry for Peace* (Breakthru Publications) and *Anthology of Little Magazine Poets* (Asylum Publications. As Tina Cryer she writes teenage pony novels (published by Forelock Books).

Taffy Nyawanza is a Zimbabwean lawyer and writer who lives in the UK. His short fiction has appeared in *Afritondo, The National Flash Fiction Journal, The JHHF Review, The Untitled: Voice Anthology, Kalahari Review, Lumiere Review, Per Happened Mag, Jalada Africa* and *MIROnline*. He is on the Exiled Writers Ink programme for his debut chapbook which will be published in early 2021.

Nasrin Parvaz became a civil rights activist when the Islamic regime took power in 1979. She was arrested in 1982 and spent eight years in prison. Her books are *One Woman's Struggle in Iran, A Prison Memoir,* and *The Secret Letters from X to A* (Victorina Press 2018). Nasrin's poetry and stories have been published in different anthologies. Her paintings were accepted for inclusion in the exhibitions, Calendar and for postcards. http://nasrinparvaz.org/, https://members.tortoisemedia.com/2020/09/09/evin-prison-wednesday-photo-essay-paintings/content.html?fbclid=IwAR2jA2ZtW_E6o5eckuPyTXwVPTK4y2omctxO9T8zrVhcckiHOIIb6PRD6uI

Helen Pizzey holds an MA in Creative Writing from Bath Spa and her short collection, *Invisibility for Beginners*, is published by Cinnamon Press. In collaboration with Irish composer Ian Wilson, she has also had poems set to music and broadcast on Radio 3. She was awarded Highly Commended in this year's Brian Dempsey Memorial Competition and lives on the edge of Poole Harbour, close to RSPB Arne.

Mary Powell is from Northern Ireland and lives in London with her husband. She worked as a Clinical Nurse Specialist, in various Mental Health settings. She has an MA in Poetry Writing, from Newcastle University/The Poetry School, London. She is interested in the energies that gather in the arena of a poem and what those energies give to the reader.

Sue Proffitt lives by the coast in South Devon. Writing poetry is central to her life and is an exploration of the beauty and mystery of the more-than-human world, and of our complex human relationship with it. Her second collection, *The Lock-Picker*, will be coming out late this year, published by Palewell Press. In 2018 she was awarded a Hawthornden Fellowship.

David Punter has published seven collections of poetry, and had individual poems placed in a wide range of magazines, including *PN Review*, *Agenda* and *The Rialto*. His last professional post was as Professor of Poetry at the University of Bristol, UK, and his most recent poetry collection, *Those Other Fields*, was published by Palewell earlier this year; also in 2020 a poem of his was long-listed in the National Poetry Competition.

Liba Ravindran is a 29 year old poet from Sri Lankan Tamil heritage, born in Norway and presently living in Southgate, North London. He has been writing for five years with a breadth of material spanning poetry, essays, short stories and a play. Liba has been a regular attendee of Enfield Poets for a few years now, and involved in the local poetry/spoken word scene in London through readings at various venues. He has been recognised for his work through winning competitions, being published in anthologies and being a booked performer. The content is ironically quixotic and surreally perceptive in its philosophical themes covering dreams, love, reality and nature.

Camilla Reeve is a writer, independent publisher and organic gardener. She has 4 poetry collections: *Travels of a Spider* 2006; *Travelling East by Road and Soul* (flipped eye publishing, 2009); *Raft of Puffins*, 2016; and *Tales from Two Cities*, 2018; and enjoys performing her work live. Her YA futuristic fantasy, *The Cloud Singer*, is about global warming and she is working on its sequel. In 2016, after 30 years in IT, she founded Palewell Press, publishing books on Justice, Equality and Sustainability. Palewell Press is a founding member of the Changing Wor(l)ds Network of cultural activists.

Richard Reid was born in 1945. An early interest in computers led to a career that took him all over the UK and Europe. Arthur Ransome's books introduced him to sailing, and to the Norfolk Broads, where he and his wife, Pat, made their home on retirement. Words and music, his other lifelong interests, have made him a bass recorder player and occasional hymn writer in a church band and a village magazine columnist.

Loraine Saacks was born in London a few days after Pearl Harbour was attacked in 1941. First years in Sidcup, Kent – and the Chislehurst Caves, overnight. Attended Waverley House Primary School, and, later, Babington House in Eltham. Did secretarial work on the Editorial Floor of the *Sunday Mirror* and much later *'Woman's Journal'*. Awarded The Marsh Award 2006-2007 for outstanding achievement in Bachelor of Science (Hons) Health. Recent work published in Mslexia, Live Canon and, shortlisted in first twenty, of Writers and Year Book's short story competition, in 2016

Rachel Sambrooks is a writer and parent/carer who was gigging as a stand-up comic and performance poet until the Covid-19 lockdown. She has three collections with her latest Harpy being published by Palewell Press.

Barbara Saunders is an English teacher, currently writing about BLM and refugees. Two BLM poems will be published by Civic

Leicester, a poem for refugees appears online (Exiled Ink, 2019) and in a fund-raiser for refugees, *Over Land Over Sea* (Five Leaves, 2016) which was translated into Italian and Rumanian. Ekphrastik poems appear in *A Farewell to Art: Chagall, Shakespeare and Prospero* (Ben Uri Gallery, 2018) and *Writing on Glass* (HLF Sutton Archives, 2018).

A.V. Shepherd is a writer, teacher, and education scholar presently dividing her time between the UK and the US. As well as poetry, she enjoys both academic and non-fiction writing and has been published in a number of magazines, including *The Times Educational Supplement.* In the spare time she finds outside of doing a PhD, she is working on her first book.

Jane Sherwin is already proud to be a Palewell Press Author. Palewell published her 85 plus poetry book, Grandmother's Patchwork, on Jane's 85th birthday, last November. It's been selling well (despite Covid) and she is most grateful to Palewell's chief editor for all the careful nurturing that her book has had.

Michael Tanner was born in Bristol in 1933. After National Service with the King's African Rifles, he taught in secondary schools for 38 years. He has helped to bring up five children. His poems have been included in many anthologies. He has had one novel published, *The Fogou Episode* and, very recently, a collection of poems, *Elemental,* Palewell Press. He has written many articles on the environment and ecology.

Valerie Tigwell began writing in her 20's and has been published in several poetry magazines; winning three national competitions. She has recorded poems for 'County Sound' and won first prize for a National Poetry Day poetry competition held by Berkshire Radio. Valerie is a member of Wey Poets, postal folios, and the Civil Service Poetry Workshop, and has edited 'WAVES' their poetry magazine.

Margaret Whittock is a retired academic. Having written and published extensively during her career as a sociologist, she now concentrates mainly on creative writing, in addition to developing her lifelong love of drawing and painting. She has independently published three novels in varying genres, including Historical, Noir, and Young Adult Fiction, and is currently writing short stories and poems, a number of which have been recently published. Although Margaret now lives in London she grew up and lived a great deal of her adult life in Northern Ireland, in the shadow of the beautiful Mourne Mountains. The folklore and mystical quality of her homeland continue to influence much of her writing and artwork, as does her wide experience of living and working abroad, particularly in Turkey and West Africa, where she spent long periods of time. Further details of Margaret's work can be found on her website, *Dark Mourne Press*: http://www.darkmournepress.com

Kim Whysall-Hammond is a Londoner living in a small country town in Southern England. An expert in obsolete telecommunications arcana, Kim believes, against all evidence, that she is a good dancer. Her poetry has appeared in *Ink, Sweat and Tears, Amaryllis, Allegro, Fourth and Sycamore, The Blue Nib, London Grip, Marble* and *Crannóg* among others. She shares poetry at thecheesesellerswife@wordpress.com and is a Best of the Net nominee.

Rosemary Wolfson likes to write poetic prose, sometimes for performance art. She has participated in Open Mic sessions at Brook's bookshop, Pinner, and the Poetry Society, Covent Garden. She has done courses in drama and art, both of which influence her writing style. Rosemary gained a BA Hons in Art History as a mature student.

Sholeh Wolpé is an Iranian-born poet and playwright. Wolpé's literary work includes over twelve collections of poetry, books of translations, and anthologies, as well as several plays. She is the recipient of the 2014 PEN/Heim, 2013 Midwest Book Award, 2010 Lois Roth Persian Translation prize, and her most recent books include *Keeping Time With Blue Hyacinth*, and *The Conference of the Birds* (W.W. Norton). She is the current Writer-in-Residence at UC Irvine. www.sholehwolpe.com

George Wright is a Londoner of the blitz era. His career has been in local authority social work, mainly in adult mental health. He has been a member of Croydon Poets Anonymous for 20 years and gets encouragement from his wife Irma, who has also been published by Palewell Press.

Palewell Press

Palewell Press is an independent publisher handling poetry, fiction and non-fiction with a focus on books that foster Justice, Equality and Sustainability. The Editor can be reached on enquiries@palewellpress.co.uk

www.ingramcontent.com/pod-product-compliance
Lightning Source LLC
Chambersburg PA
CBHW071014180726
48291CB00004B/1455

* 9 7 8 1 9 1 1 5 8 7 4 5 3 *